IN PERFORMANCE

IN PERFORMANCE

Contemporary Monologues
for Men and Women
Late Thirties to Forties

JV Mercanti

Applause Theatre & Cinema Books
An Imprint of Hal Leonard Corporation

Published in 2016 by Applause Theatre & Cinema Books
An Imprint of Hal Leonard Corporation
7777 West Bluemound Road
Milwaukee, WI 53213

Trade Book Division Editorial Offices
33 Plymouth St., Montclair, NJ 07042

Printed in the United States of America

Book design by Mark Lerner
Composition by UB Communications

Library of Congress Cataloging-in-Publication Data is available upon request.

www.applausebooks.com

CONTENTS

MEN'S MONOLOGUES

WOMEN'S MONOLOGUES

PREFACE

One of the best auditions I've ever seen was for Roundabout Theatre Company's 2001 revival of Stephen Sondheim and James Goldman's musical *Follies*. Jim Carnahan, the casting director, and I had called in Judith Ivey for the role of Sally Durant Plummer. If you don't know who Judith Ivey is, please Google her immediately. You have most likely seen her in something on stage, in film, or on television. You might also have seen a production that she's directed. She is a prolific artist.

The role of Sally Durant Plummer is fragile and complex. Sally has been married to Buddy for years, but all that time she has been pining for the love of Ben Stone, who is (unhappily) married to Sally's former best friend, Phyllis. Sally is going crazy with love and desire that has been burning for over twenty years.

Ms. Ivey was asked to prepare a cut from Sally's famous first-act song "In Buddy's Eyes," an aria through which she tries to convince Ben, in order to make him jealous, that she's deliriously happy in her life with Buddy. She was also asked to prepare a short scene from the show. Present in the room for the audition were Stephen Sondheim, the composer and lyricist; Matthew Warchus, the director; Todd Haimes, artistic director; Jim Carnahan, casting director; Paul Ford, the accompanist; a reader; and myself.

Walking into the room as herself, Ms. Ivey conversed with Mr. Warchus and Mr. Sondheim about her career and, very briefly, about the character. She then took a moment with Paul Ford to discuss the music. Following that, she came to the center of the playing space, closed her eyes, took a deep breath, and prepared herself to begin acting. In that moment of preparation, which truly lasted no longer than a breath, her body changed, her physicality changed, the very air around her seemed to change. She took the character into her body. Ms. Ivey then opened her eyes, nodded at Mr. Ford, and began to sing.

Ms. Ivey executed the song with specificity, a rich but contained emotional connection to the material, a strong objective, carefully thought-out actions, and a deep understanding of this woman and her desire. She went directly from the song to the scene, completely off-book (lines memorized), and when she finished—the room was silent. Mr. Sondheim had tears in his eyes. Mr. Warchus didn't have a word of direction to give her. It was not that Ms. Ivey had provided us with a complete performance. No, not at all. She had shown us the possibility of what she could create. She had shown us the potential of her Sally Durant Plummer. Her point of view was clear, consistent, and deeply, deeply affecting.

"Thank you, Judith. That was wonderful," Matthew Warchus finally said.

"I really love Sally," she responded, "But I was wondering if you might also consider me for the role of Phyllis. I've prepared that material as well."

"Of course I would. Would you like a few minutes to go outside and prepare?" he asked.

"No. No, that's all right. I can do it right now," she responded.

And after saying this, Ms. Ivey closed her eyes. She very slowly turned away from us, put her hair up in a tight bun, and turned around to face the room. It took no longer than thirty seconds, but once again her body, her posture, the way she related to the air around her, had changed. The atmosphere of the room shifted with her. Once again, she nodded to Paul Ford at the piano, and she fearlessly launched into the Phyllis Stone material.

It was astonishing. Not a false note was sung or uttered. Ivey had such a deep understanding of the cold facade Phyllis wears in order to cover up her broken heart and broken dreams. Phyllis is the polar opposite of Sally: cool, controlled, calculating, and hard.

Ms. Ivey thanked us for the opportunity. We thanked her for her work. The room remained still and silent for a while after she left.

Without a doubt, Mr. Warchus knew he must cast her in the show. She landed the role of Sally Durant Plummer.

It was clear that Ms. Ivey did a very thorough study of the text in preparation for this audition. She understood who these characters were at their very core; how they thought; why they spoke the way they did, using language in their own individual and specific way. She understood how they moved, where they held their weight, how they related to the space around them. Most importantly, she understood the characters' objectives (what they wanted) and how to use the other person in the scene to get what she wanted. Finally, Ivey was excited to show us how she could portray these women. She wasn't concerned about getting it "right." She managed to accomplish this while bringing herself to the character instead of the other way around.

More recently, I was casting the Broadway revival of *Romeo and Juliet* starring Orlando Bloom and Condola Rashād. The process of making this production happen is a book in and of itself. It was in development for over three years.

I flew to Los Angeles to work with Mr. Bloom in June 2012. We spent a week going through the text, talking about objectives, tactics, and actions. We discussed the relationships between Romeo and the other characters in the play in connection to his main objective, which we defined, simply, as "to fly towards the sun."

Wait. Why isn't his objective about Juliet, you ask? His super-objective cannot be about Juliet, because, upon Romeo's first entrance in the play, he hasn't even *seen* her yet. He can't come on stage playing to win someone he doesn't even know. But if you perform a careful analysis of the text, you will find a plethora of both sun and flying imagery. Once he finds Juliet, she becomes his sun. This is why it's helpful as an actor to jot down the recurring themes or images you come across when reading a play you're working on, even if you're only focusing on a monologue from a larger text. This is also why it's important to pay attention to the *words* the playwright uses.

Bloom is a physical actor, and we spent a lot of time playing on our feet, finding the scenes through physical action as well as language. Getting Romeo into his body helped get Bloom out of his head. Also, the very simple and stimulating objective—to fly towards the sun—gave him a place to start from that sparked his imagination, was very actable, and influenced his physical life. His heart was always open and reaching up.

I worked with Bloom again in NYC for a few days, and then he flew to London to audition for David Leveaux, our director. He landed the role. That was in July 2012.

We did an initial round of casting in July and August of that year, seeing actors for a variety of the supporting roles. As we were securing official dates (as well as a Juliet!), we could only audition actors and tell them we were interested in them. We couldn't make offers. We couldn't tell them actual production dates. We couldn't tell them anything for certain, not even who our Romeo was. Many of these actors were not officially called back until January 2013, which is when Ms. Rashād (whose first audition was in August) landed the Juliet role after four auditions in New York and one in Los Angeles with Bloom.

Some actors never even had a callback. I was in constant contact with agents and managers from July 2012 to May 2013, letting them know we were still interested in their clients; that there might or might not be another round of callbacks; that they should let me know immediately if their client had another job offer, et cetera. And all the while, I was auditioning new people for parts we hadn't seen earlier. The show required a cast of twenty-three on-stage actors and one off-stage standby for Bloom.

Putting the Capulet and Montague families together was like a puzzle: headshots spread out on a long folding table as we weighed the pros of each actor, their look, and their qualities. All of these factors influence the production as a whole. Official offers were not made until May 2013.

I tell you this to illustrate how you, the actor, never know what goes on behind the scenes. Ultimately, you have no power over it. The only power you have is how you present yourself to the room as a person and a performer.

With rehearsal quickly approaching in July 2013, we had one role left to cast: Sampson, a servant of the House of Capulet. The actor playing this part would also understudy Justin Guarini, who played Paris. By the time we were in final callbacks for this small role, I had prescreened (an audition with just the actor and casting director, preceding a director's callback) or checked the availability of some four hundred actors for the part. Four hundred actors for a role that had approximately three lines of dialogue.

David Leveaux is attracted to actors who have strong personalities and who bring that into the room. The male casting for this production depended on virile, strong, playful men who also happened to be skilled in speaking verse, as David puts it, "on the line." That means speaking the lines as written and not adding unnecessary pauses or breaks in between every thought or word, allowing the action of the line to take you to the poetry instead of vice versa.

Our Sampson, a young man by the name of Donte Bonner, was all of these things and more. He walked into the room calm, collected, and in control. He enjoyed the process of auditioning. Bonner was excited to show us what he could do with the role, not preoccupied with hoping we liked him. This attitude is immediately attractive in an actor. On top of this, Bonner brought his own unique point of view to the character he was reading for. He was simple, specific and alive. He was also skilled at taking direction. Although he had a very strong idea of his own, he was able to adjust when David asked for something completely different.

You can achieve the same level of performance as Ms. Ivey or Mr. Bonner if you put the requisite amount of work into your monologue, ask yourself the right questions (and the questions I ask you to examine following each of the pieces in this book), and activate your imagination.

Introduction
Approaching the Monologue

Actors are interpretive storytellers. We often forget that.

You take the words the writer has given you and process them through your own unique instrument (your mind, your body, your imagination, and, hopefully, your heart and your soul), and you turn those words into action—into doing. I'm sure you've been taught by this point in your career that acting is doing. As a teacher, acting coach, and director, I am constantly asking the questions "What are you doing?" and "Why are you doing that?" This doesn't mean a *physical* action. It means how are you *actively pursuing* your objective?

I'm also always asking the question "What does that mean?"

Most beginning actors think that memorizing the lines is enough. Or that emoting is enough. As I tell my undergraduate students, acting is hard work, and it's more than just memorizing lines and saying them out loud. It takes emotional connection, analytical skill, and an understanding of human behavior and relationships—as well as a relationship with language—to turn the written word into honest, believable action. Remember, any playwright worth his/her salt takes great care in choosing the language a character uses. In a well-written play, each character speaks differently. It is your job to find the key to unlocking the meaning of that language while giving it your own personal spin.

Rehearsing a monologue is tricky business, because you don't physically have a partner in front of you to work off of, react to, and actually affect. Oftentimes you'll find yourself staring at an empty chair, saying the lines out loud over and over. Hopefully, what follows will help you deepen your rehearsal process and activate your imagination. Imagination is one of the strongest abilities an actor can possess. If you can enter a room and create a specific, believable world in two minutes, we will trust that you can sustain that world for two-plus hours on a stage or in front of a camera.

You're reading this book because you're looking for an audition piece. It might be for a nonequity or community-theater production, an undergraduate or graduate program, or a professional meeting with an agent or casting director. It may even be for an EPA.[1] Whatever the case, you're looking for a piece that—I hope—you feel you connect with on some level; that expresses a particular essence of you; that shows off your sense of humor or sense of self; and that, above all, tells a story you want to tell.

Your monologue choice tells the person (or sometimes the numerous people) behind the table something about you. Certainly it lets us know that you can stand in front of an audience, comfortable in your own body, and perform. It tells us you can open your mouth and speak someone else's words with meaning, confidence, and a sense of ease. It lets us know whether or not you have the ability to project or modify your voice depending on the requirements of the space.

More than that, your monologue choice tells us something about who you are as a person. Your monologue can tell us the type of things you respond to emotionally, intellectually, and humorously. After all, we're going under the assumption that you put a lot of time and care into finding a piece that you wanted to perform. You took

---

1   EPA stands for Equity Principal Auditions. All productions that produce on a contract with Actors Equity Association are required to have these calls. The casting department for these EPAs can provide scenes from the play they are casting or request monologues.

the time to commit that piece to memory and to heart. You've imbued it with your sense of humor, understanding, compassion, pain, and so on. More than just telling us whether or not you can act—and a monologue is by no means the only arbiter of this—the monologue helps us decide if we like you as a person, if you're someone we want to work with, study with, teach, and hire.

The monologue is, then, a reflection of you. What do you want us to know about you? This is why not every monologue works for every actor. Choose carefully. If it doesn't feel right, it most likely isn't. If you think it's a possibility, commit to the piece, do all of the work you can on it, and then perform it for people whose opinions you trust—not just people who tell you everything you do is wonderful (as nice as it is to have those people around). Ask someone who can be honest and helpfully critical.

Our first impulse is to ask, "Did you like it? How was I?"

Unfortunately, "like" is subjective. I can *not* like something yet still be affected by it. Instead, ask questions such as the following: "What did you learn about me from that? What do you think it says about who I am? What was the story? Could you tell what my objective was? Who was I? Did I take you on a journey? Was it playing on different levels, or did it seem too one-note?"

Then take it to a more businesslike level from there: "What am I selling? Does it play to my strengths? What weaknesses are on display in this piece? Does it seem 'type'-appropriate? Did I display a sense of strength as well as vulnerability?"

I will discuss some of these issues further in the pages that follow. However, it's important for an actor of any age to realize that you are selling yourself, and so you need to think like a businessperson. Play to your strengths and overcome your weaknesses. And if you can't overcome your weaknesses, learn how to cover them up! For example, if you can't cry on cue, don't pick a piece that requires you to do so.

If you're terrible at telling jokes, don't end your monologue on a punch line.

So, you're a storyteller, an interpreter, and a businessperson. I told you acting was hard work. Pursue this career with an open heart and a tough skin, because for all the applause you'll receive, you'll also receive a lot of criticism and rejection. You have no control over why you did or didn't get cast. You do have control over your performance in the room. Focus on telling the story, a story you connect deeply to, and that's a safe and sure foundation.

Now let's begin.

Why Monologues?

Monologues give us a sense of your skill level and your personality.

As a professional casting director, I can think of only two instances in which I've asked actors to prepare a monologue for an audition. The first was when casting the Broadway production of Andrew Lloyd Webber's musical *The Woman in White*, directed by Trevor Nunn. All the actors coming into the room, whether auditioning for a leading role or a place in the ensemble, were asked to prepare music from the show, a contrasting song of their choice, and a Shakespearean monologue. Mr. Nunn, a Shakespearean expert, used the monologue as a way to get to know the actors, direct them, and gauge their ability to handle language and to play objectives and actions. I received a number of calls from agents, managers, and actors saying that they were uncomfortable with Shakespeare and maybe they shouldn't come in. However, I assured them this was the way Mr. Nunn worked, and he wouldn't be judging the actors' ability to handle the language requirements of Shakespeare but rather their ability to tell a story and take direction.

The second instance was when casting the Broadway revival of *Cyrano de Bergerac*. David Leveaux, the director, asked the men coming in for smaller roles, such as the poets and the soldiers, to prepare a classical monologue. In this instance, casting *was* dependent on the actors' ability to handle classical language. We were also able to assign understudy roles from these auditions because, based on the actors' monologue choices, we had a sense of who they were and of their technical and emotional abilities.

Now, that's two instances of using monologues in a more than fifteen-year career in casting. Truth to tell, I don't like monologue auditions. Although they give me a sense of who you are, they don't tell me if you can really act. I know some great actors who are terrible with monologues, and vice versa. Real acting is about collaboration. The true test of an actor is how they perform when faced with a director, another cast member, scenic and lighting elements, props, et cetera. You can be a brilliant performer when on your own and completely crash and burn when faced with a partner to whom you need to be open and receptive.

Nonetheless, as a college professor, I've learned that monologues are very important. Actors use them to audition for a program; we use them for season auditions within the department; and most importantly, my graduating seniors are asked to perform their monologues when they meet with agents and managers after their showcase.

Why? For all the reasons I've previously stated: Do you have the ability to speak with confidence and clarity? Do you have the ability to create a two-minute storytelling and emotional arc? Are you comfortable in your body? Can you play an objective? Can you play an action? Are you in control of your emotional life? Are you someone I want to spend time and work with? A monologue lets us know *who you are*. So it's important that you *know* who you are. And you don't have to be *one* thing, but again, know your strengths.

There appears to be an unwritten rule in schools that urges people away from "storytelling" monologues. In my experience, though, people are at their most active, engaged, and emotionally connected when they are sharing a personal experience. In this book you will find storytelling monologues for this very reason. What you must keep in mind in the performing of them is that we tell stories for a reason. Through these stories, the characters are trying to tell us something about themselves. Therefore, you're telling us something about *you* when you perform it. It's up to you to decide what that is, but make certain you feel emotionally connected to the piece and that you keep it active and engaged with a clear objective.

Now, in the monologues that don't necessarily contain an obvious "story," what do I mean by "storytelling"? I mean you are giving us a brief glimpse into the larger story of that character. You are living out the experience of—bringing to life—a very specific instance in the life of that character. Your plotting of that experience still needs to have a beginning, middle, and end. You must chart your emotional arc for these pieces just as you would if it were a traditional story. Take us on a journey, just the same.

CAUTION: Try not to beat us over the head by living in one extreme emotion for two minutes and simply playing one tactic the entire time. If you do this, your monologue will become monotonous and we will stop listening. Inexperienced actors sometimes think that simply crying or yelling or any generalized emoting is acting. If the character is still talking, it means they haven't achieved their objective yet. And if they haven't achieved their objective yet, it means that they haven't exhausted their arsenal of tactics yet. And if they haven't, you haven't.

Choosing a Monologue

I hope you've come to this book as a starting point. The best way to choose a monologue is to read plays. Read lots and lots of plays. Read every play you can get your hands on. Watch movies and television shows. Searching for—and preparing—monologues requires lots of work. Also, it's your job.

Why should you do all this work? The reasons are plenty, but let me expound upon a few of them.

1. Playwrights are the reason we, as theater professionals, exist. It is our job to honor their work while bringing it to life. You will soon find yourself gravitating to a certain writer or writers. You will want to perform their work. You will seek out productions of theirs wherever you are in the country or the world. You will, eventually, want to work with this playwright and help create new work or revive previous work. You will want to interpret and tell their stories. And—if you move to a city like New York, Los Angeles, or Chicago—you will most likely come into contact with them at some point in time and you can speak with them about their work with knowledge and breadth.

   Conversely, there will be writers you find you don't connect with at all. If this is the case, do not use monologues from their work. You need to love the piece on some very basic level. So even if you can't define why you're not a fan, move on. Pick up the play a few months or years later and read it again. Maybe you'll come at it from a different perspective and it will connect with you. It may never.

   Finally, many of these playwrights you love and admire get hired to write, produce, and run television shows. Whether in New York or L.A., you will come across a writer who has moved from theater to the film industry for any number of reasons (money). You will find, I bet, their heart still remains in the theater, and they will love to hear you are a fan of theirs.

2. You may have come across monologues that weren't right for you earlier in your life but that could be put on the shelf and pulled out again as you've reached your late twenties and early

thirties and forties. You may still have some in reserve for when you reach your fifties and sixties—as you may have noticed, people in their fifties and sixties still audition, no matter who they are. The work, if you're lucky, never ends."

3. When you read these plays and watch TV shows and films, you're researching. You're finding out which actors are getting cast in the parts you want to play. Follow their careers. This is how you begin to track and define your "type." This is how you learn what parts are out there for you. The cast list that precedes the play in most published work is a guide for you. Google the actors and find out who they are and what they've done.

The actress Saidah Arrika Ekulona (you don't know who she is? Google her. It's your job) spoke to my students recently and said, "Don't worry about so much about your type. Don't obsess about it. Somebody, somewhere is ready to put you in a box, so why should you do it for yourself?" I wholeheartedly agree—and disagree—with her! Here's where I agree: of course you must believe you can do anything, play any part. You need to constantly raise the bar for yourself so that you have goals to work toward. Just because you're the "leading lady" or "leading man" doesn't mean you can't also find the humor, sexuality, and hunger in those roles. You need to find the complexities and polarities in every role you play. People are complicated, and therefore so are characters.

However, you also need to keep in mind that this is a business. And people in business want to know how you're marketable. So if you have a list of actors who are doing the things you know how to do, playing the parts you know you can play, you are armed with information that's going to help you market yourself. Don't think of defining your type as a "box." It's not. It's a marketing strategy.

It may sound like a cliché, but knowledge is power. And your knowledge of these plays, writers, and fellow actors is your weapon. Put it to use.

4. Films and TV are fair game when searching for material. However, you want to stay away from material that would be considered "iconic." Avoid characters that are firmly ingrained in our popular culture. Shows like *Girls*, *Sex and the City*, or *Friends* have great writing, but that writing became more and more tailored to the specific actors playing those roles as the seasons progressed. It is difficult to approach that material without hearing the voices of those original actors in our heads. So enjoy those shows, but don't use them, even if your type is a Carrie, a Charlotte, a Joey, or a Chandler.

5. Sometimes you'll find a character that you really like but who doesn't have a stand-alone monologue in the play. You'll be tempted to cut and paste the lines together until you form it into something that seems complete. I caution you away from this. Although some of the pieces in this book have been edited, there has been no major cutting and rearranging. I find that it destroys the author's intent. You're crafting a piece into something it wasn't meant to be. Look at something else by this writer. Or search for a similar character in another play. Your "type" work will come in handy here. The actor who played this role was also in what other plays? This writer has also written what other plays?

6. Once you've chosen a monologue from this book (or from a play or film), please read the entire work. Then read it again. Then—read it again. Although you will ultimately be performing the piece out of context, you can act it well only if you can make sense of the context in which it was written.

Preparing the Monologue

I am asking you to do a lot of work here. But if this monologue leads to landing a job or an agent or gets you into the grad school of your choice, then you want to do as much preparation as possible to make it a complete, worthwhile experience for you and the people behind the table.

I've heard from many actors over the years that they don't want to be "over-rehearsed." They want to keep their piece "fresh." If you feel your piece is over-rehearsed, then you are doing something wrong. There is no such thing. The amount of work that goes into keeping a piece fresh and alive is endless. Ask someone who has been in a Broadway show for six months, or a year. There is always something more to unearth in a role, especially if you keep clarifying and refining your objective, actions, and relationships.

Here's how to start.

1. Read the entire play.
2. Read the entire play again.
3. Read it one more time.
4. Although you will have been very tempted to do so, do *not* read the monologue out loud yet. You've read the play a few times now, and you're beginning to, consciously or unconsciously, realize the intention of the piece in the whole.
5. Have a notebook handy to write down your initial thoughts, reactions, and responses to the play, the characters, and the relationships.

I want you to think about the play as a whole, first, by asking these questions:

Is this a dramatic or a comedic monologue?

This is a tough question. I find that most good monologues walk the line between the two, putting them in the "seriocomic" category. A comedic monologue is not always about landing a joke. A comedic monologue shows that you can handle material that is light and playful while still playing a strong objective and having an emotional connection to the text. A dramatic monologue tackles more serious issues, events, and emotions. Be careful that your dramatic monologue doesn't dissolve into you screaming and/or crying in the direction of the auditioner. This is *not* a sign that you can act. If you're crying and screaming, then you are most likely not playing toward an objective while using strong actions. You're just being self-indulgent.

In life, we rarely get what we want when we scream or cry at people. It's no different in acting.

What are some of the major themes of the play?

It is often easiest to define your character's objective by wording it to include the main themes or images in the play.

Themes are the major ideas or topics of the play, together with the writer's point of view on these topics. Sometimes the theme will reveal itself through repetition of imagery, such as the sun and flight imagery I mentioned earlier in *Romeo and Juliet*.

Make a list of these themes, both major and minor, in your notebook.

What does the title of the play mean?

The author's intention or point of view is often most clearly defined in the title of the play. Thinking about it might also lead you to define the main theme of the work, as just discussed. Your work on the theme of the play should lead you directly here.

Who is the main character in the play?

Whose story is it? What is their journey? If you're performing a monologue of the main character, how does the piece affect their progression? If you're performing a piece from a supporting character, how does it assist or impede the main character's journey?

The main character is the person who takes the biggest journey over the course of the play. Your monologue is one of the following: (1) the person on that journey; (2) a person helping the main character on that journey; (3) a person creating an obstacle to the main character achieving their goal.

Even in an ensemble play, there is always a main character.

What is your objective?

This question is twofold, because I'm asking you to define your objective for both the play and the monologue. You need to define what this character wants throughout the entire play—from the moment he or she steps onto the stage. Then you need to define how this two-minute (or so) piece fits into the whole.

An objective is a *simple, active, positive* statement that defines the journey your character is on.

It is in defining an objective that many actors tend to hinder their performance. You never want to define your objective in the following ways: (1) I want "to *be* something," or (2) I want "to *feel* something." These are passive, inactive statements in which you will not make any forward progression. Emotion does play a role in acting, but not when it comes to defining an objective.

Instead I want you to define it in very vivid, active words that inspire you and spark your imagination. This is where your knowledge of the entire play and the character you are creating comes into action.

Begin by thinking in very primal terms. Objectives should hold life-or-death stakes: companionship, shelter, protection, nourishment, sex, fight, and flight.

"I want to hold my family together" is a very strong objective.

"I want to make someone love me" is another.

However, I challenge you to take it a step further. If you're working on Joan Ackermann's *Stanton's Garage*, you might start with "I want to get out of the garage." But you can use the language and the imagery from the play, taking your objective into deeper territory: "I want to fix all the things about me that are broken so I can drive safely away." The more vividly you can paint the objective, especially by using words and images from the play itself, the better.

Play your objective with the belief that you're going to WIN! Play positive choices. We don't go to the theater to see people lose. We want to see them try to overcome. Even if they don't succeed.

I can't stress enough that every time you step in front of someone to act, you must have an objective. Every time. Whether you're performing a monologue, a song, or an entire play, you must have an objective. It's one of the basic conditions of acting. If you don't have an objective, you don't have a goal, and there's no reason to act (or to watch). Even if you find out that objective doesn't work, commit to it while you're performing and then try something else the next time.

I have asked many an actor in an audition what their objective was only to get silence in return. Not every casting director is going to do this and then give you another chance. Figure out what you want to *do* before you come into the room. Otherwise, you're wasting your time and ours.

What are the beats and actions?

A *beat* is a transition: a change in thought, action, subject, or tactic.

Not every line is a new beat. Try to find it organically. When it feels like there is a shift in thought, there most likely is. That is your beat. Trust your instincts. Are you accomplishing what you want? Are you winning? If not, it's time to shift your tactic.

Have you been playing the same tactic over and over without achieving your goal? It's time to shift your tactic. Backtrack: when did that start? How can you adjust?

Actions are active verbs that define what you are doing in any particular moment. Meaning, you attach an active verb to every line of text: to sway, to punish, to defend, to challenge, and so on.

Actions become your roadmap, your markers. If you're a musician, think of them as musical notes. The note is written there, but it's up to you to color it, make it your own, and endow it with meaning. Engage your own unique point of view to make it personal. However, every new action does not necessarily mean you've come to a beat change. Again, feel it out instinctively. You should have an action for every line. Hard work, I know. However, this work makes you really pay attention to the language of the play and the words you are using to achieve your objective.

You cannot consciously play these objectives, beats, actions, and tactics, but you must rehearse with them in mind so that you can internalize them. Once they've become internalized, they will play themselves. It's a form of muscle memory. The challenge then becomes to trust that the work is there and let it go.

Check in with your (imaginary) scene partner. Make sure your actions are landing. This is where your imagination comes into play. When you look at the empty space you have to see how they're reacting, how they're looking (or not looking) at you.

Playing actions helps in two areas: it helps you do more than play the "mood" of the piece. Mood is established in the arc of the story-telling, not in the way you say the lines. Mood is also established in how you're relating to the other person: are you winning, or losing? Secondly, playing actions will help you not play the end of the monologue at the beginning. If the monologue ends in death, you don't want us to know that when you start. Take us there without letting us know we're going to get there.

When I was working as the assistant director of Martin Mc-Donagh's Broadway production of A *Behanding in Spokane*, John Crowley, the director, would sit at the table with the actors every afternoon after lunch and make them assign actions to every line of text. We did this for weeks. It is oftentimes very frustrating, but it lets you know where you're going. It forces you into specificity. And if any particular action doesn't seem to work for you, throw it out and try another! That is why actors rehearse.

Right now maybe you're asking yourself why you need to do all of this work. Let's go back to the words that opened this book: Actors are storytellers, and the best stories are those told with specificity. Think of this monologue as a smaller story inside a larger one. You need to understand the larger story the playwright is telling in order to tell this shorter story. You need to know the details in order to bring them to life.

The greater your understanding of the piece as a whole, the better your ability to interpret it. Doing all of this work doesn't take all the fun out of performing. The more information we have, the deeper we can go and the more fun we can have. Specificity leads to freedom.

Remember, people rarely expect to speak in monologue form. Have an expectation of how you think your (unseen) partner may react. This is part of a conversation, and your partner is letting you speak for quite a bit of time, or you are not letting them get a word in. Don't approach it as a monologue; approach it as dialogue. Expect your scene partner to cut you off. Your expectation is key to why you go on for some two minutes. Pay attention to and play with your partner. Oftentimes this expectation of interruption will help you bring a sense of urgency to the piece.

Inevitably, you will be performing these monologues for someone who knows the play. You want your acting of the monologue to be consistent with the tone, theme, and style of the play, as well as the character's objective within it. You can't take a monologue from *Macbeth*, for example, and mine it for high comic potential. You'll look foolish, and the casting director will assume you don't know what you're doing.

Who is your character?

Once you've answered all of the above questions, it's time to start putting this person into your body.

1. What do they look like?
2. How do they dress?
3. How do they stand?
4. Where is their center of gravity?
5. How do they take up space?
6. What's their posture?
7. Where does their voice sit (i.e., head, throat, chest, diaphragm, etc.)?
8. Where do they hold tension?
9. How do they walk, sit, and stand?

It's up to you to find this person in your body—experiment with them. Holding on to what you know about them from the script, and your very strong objective, you'll be able to find physicality for them through your knowledge of them.

If you can imagine them, you can become them.

Whom is your character talking to?

These are monologues, but you need to have a very specific picture of *whom* you are talking to, because it plays directly into *why* you are talking (your objective). Some of these monologues are to a specific person, or persons; some were written as audience address. You still need to decide to whom, specifically, it is directed and have a clear image of that person.

Place that person somewhere in the room with you. You should never perform your monologue directly to the person for whom you are auditioning unless they ask. You can place them, in your imagination, to the left or the right and a little in front of that person. You can place them behind that person and a little above their head. You can place them closer to you, to your immediate left, right, or center. However, make sure that they're not so close that you are forced to look down while you deliver your monologue. We need to see your face.

Now that you've placed your "acting partner" somewhere, you need to imagine what they look like.

1. What are they wearing?
2. Are they sitting, or standing?
3. What is your relationship to them?
4. What do you need from them? (This ties in to your objective)
5. How is delivering this monologue bringing you closer to achieving your goal?
6. By the end of the monologue, did you win? Did you get what you wanted? Are you closer or further away from achieving you goal?

If you can imagine them vividly and specifically, we will see them.

What's so urgent?

Less experienced actors often lack a sense of urgency. Remember, your character is dealing with life-and-death stakes! Urgent doesn't mean "do it quickly." Urgent means: why do you need to say these things right now? Why do you need to achieve your objective right now? What just happened that makes every word in this monologue so important? This should carry life-or-death stakes: *If I don't achieve this objective right now, my life will fall apart.*

Using the language to your advantage (covered in a section that follows) will guarantee that you can add heat to your monologue without rushing through.

The quality of your time on stage is much more important than the quantity. Please don't think that the longer you take, the more illustrative you're being.

Emotional Connection

Up until now I have hardly mentioned feelings, emotions, or emoting. You must, of course, have a strong emotional connection to the monologue you choose. Your connection may grow or dissipate when you complete the work outlined above. Sometimes the more you discover about a play, or a character, the further it feels from your initial response. If this is the case, and you can't reclaim that initial spark, then move on to something else. You can always find another piece.

Conversely, your initial response to the monologue might be only so-so until you do more work on it, finding yourself truly enlivened and engaged by it. In that case, take it and run.

Acting is not about emoting. Less experienced actors tend to find pieces with very high emotional stakes that often require crying or screaming in order to accomplish the storytelling. Please shy away from these. We want to see that you are emotionally connected to the material and that you know how to *control* your emotional life.

We do not want to have your emotions unleashed upon us in a flood that you cannot contain. Therefore, a monologue that occurs at the climax of a play is probably best left performed in the context of the show.

After performing all of the work laid out above, your emotional connection to the piece should be growing organically. You relationship to the character, his/her objective, the relationships, and the story should be incredibly strong. You should find yourself invested in living through the experience and sharing the story.

If you feel that you are still generating (read: *forcing*) an emotional reaction in order to make the monologue work for you, I would suggest putting it aside. You don't want us to see you working hard in order to put the material over.

Language and Point of View

I've talked a lot about your relationship to language and how you need to have one. Words and punctuation, as provided by the writer, can sometimes unlock the key to your character. Language is how these characters express what they need. Please use the words to your advantage.

Nothing about the language is secondary. If there weren't words, there wouldn't be a story.

Remember that acting occurs *on* the lines, not in between them. Try to express what you're feeling by coloring a word or a phrase with your point of view while maintaining the flow of the line. Tie your thoughts together without breaking the line apart in pieces in an attempt to highlight certain words.

The line is your thought and your action: present it completely. Try not to add moments, beats, unexpressed thoughts, and feelings in between the lines. It's not necessary. Use what the playwright has given you.

If the playwright wants you to take time somewhere, they will provide the clues. It can be as specific as them writing *pause* or *beat*.

There are other clues, though:

An ellipsis (. . .) often signifies a trailing off of thought or a search for the right thing to say.

A hyphen or dash (—) often signifies a break in thought, a cut-off thought, or a new idea.

These are basically the only times you have permission to break up the thought. Otherwise, see your energy through the entire line. Stay engaged and alive, and keep the thought moving.

A word or a line written in all caps means the author wants you to highlight that particular section, but it does not necessarily mean you need to yell and scream it.

Be aware of repetition. If a writer uses the same word or phrase repeatedly, they're trying to tell you something. How you shade that word (or don't) each time it comes up says something about the character and what they're after.

Also, pay attention to periods, question marks, exclamation points, and other basic punctuation marks. These are not arbitrary. Something delivered as a statement has a completely different meaning if it's intended to be delivered as a question. This isn't your decision to make if the writer has shown otherwise.

Point of view is how you (your character) see the world, relate to the people and objects around you, and relate to language. This is where artistry occurs. Anyone can say the words. How you give them meaning, how you filter all of this through your perspective, is what makes your interpretation unique.

Also, what is your point of view on the person to whom you're speaking? This has to go deeper than "I like him" or "I don't like her."

Who is she to you? "My sister," for example, is a surface definition. "This is the one person in the world I've shared all my secrets with my entire life" takes it a step further. "This is the one person in the world I've shared all my secrets with in my entire life, but she's never had her heart broken and doesn't understand how I'm feeling" takes it even further. More importantly, can this person help you achieve your objective, or are they standing in your way?

Your point of view must be apparent when you talk about a person or a place that has an emotional effect on you: your mother, your father, your sister, or your brother. Or you could be speaking about your childhood home or your favorite restaurant. How do you feel about them? Where in your body do you feel them when you speak about them?

Point of view is what makes the character *yours*.

Edit

You can't have everything. You can't make every moment last a lifetime. All of the tools I've provided you with are an effort to keep you active and engaged and in the moment. If you find yourself lingering over a word, a phrase, a pause, I want you to ask yourself *why*. Is it necessary? Are you staying true to the storytelling, the author's intention, and the character's objective? Will hanging out in that moment help you achieve your objective faster, better, with more urgency? Will screaming, crying, and wailing do the same? In both cases, probably not.

Finally, it's time for you to put all of the pieces together. You have all the elements of the story, and now you need to get from point A, to point B, to point C. This takes a long rehearsal process. It means experimenting with all of these elements. If something does not work, throw it away and try something else. If something seems to maybe, kind of work, hold on to it and experiment inside of that. Try doing the entire piece in a whisper and see what you learn. Try doing it at the top of your voice in a public place and see what you discover. Take risks with how you rehearse it and you might find something you never knew was there.

I strongly urge you *not* to practice these monologues in front of a mirror. It will only make you feel self-conscious, and you will put your focus and energy into how you look while you do it rather than into what you are *doing*. Instead, practice it in front of friends and family. Practice achieving your objective on them. Practice your actions on them.

You have created a roadmap, but that doesn't mean you can't take side trips. Your objective is in mind; now try a roundabout way of getting there. Remember, these are called "plays," and you should, in fact, play. Have fun.

In Performance

You are ready to perform the monologue in public. Here are a few quick tips for the audition room:

Some actors think it doesn't matter how they present themselves when they enter or exit the audition room. Your audition starts the moment the door opens and doesn't end until you leave.

1. Arrive early. At least fifteen minutes before your appointment time. You need this time to unclutter your mind, focus yourself, and relax.
2. When your name is called, close your eyes and take a deep breath in and out. Find your center.
3. Take as few of your personal items into the room as necessary. Try not to bring in your jacket, your bag, your purse, your gym clothes, and so on. Gentlemen, please take phones, keys, and loose change out of your front pockets; do not interrupt the natural line of your body.

4. Say a friendly "Hello" to the person or persons in the room, even if they seem engaged in another activity. Very often, we are writing notes about whoever just exited, but we will try to make contact and greet you, the next person entering the room, especially to see if you look like your headshot.

5. Look like your headshot.

6. Leave your bitterness, your disappointment, and your desperation outside of the door. There's no room for it in the audition. We can sense all of them. If you put your energy into your emotions instead of into telling the story, you will not get cast. This is a business, like any other, filled with unfairness and disappointments. Don't take it out on the people behind the table. Don't sabotage yourself. The only thing that matters in the work. You can bitch to your friends later. But we can sense your negativity, and we don't want it.

7. Do not advance on the table, introduce yourself, and attempt to shake hands. Keep a friendly, professional distance unless the person behind the table makes a move otherwise. We sometimes see a hundred people in one day; we can't shake everyone's hand.

8. Be nice to everyone in the room, including the reader and the accompanist. We take note of that. Remember we're looking to form an ensemble, and how you treat everyone matters. Also remember that today's accompanist is tomorrow's up-and-coming composer.

9. Do not apologize for what you're about to do or explain that you:
    a. Are sick.

    b. Have just been sick.

    c. Feel as if you're getting sick.

10. Find a comfortable space to stand, or ask for a chair if you're using one. There will almost always be a chair available for

you. It makes no difference to us whether you stand or sit, but it sometimes makes a difference to your monologue.

11. Once you're in position, please introduce yourself and let us know the title of the play from which the monologue comes.

12. Take a moment before you begin. Close your eyes or turn away from us. Center yourself. Runners don't hit the track and begin running. They take their position, they focus themselves, they wait for the gun, and then they go. In this situation, you are in charge of the gun. The room is yours when you walk in. As you arrived some fifteen minutes before entering the room, this shouldn't take more than a second or two. Please, no slumping in place, no shaking out your arms and legs, no vocalizing. All of this should be done at home or outside the room. The moment before is simply to focus.

13. Act! Have fun. We want you to be good. We want to welcome you into our program, our school, and our cast. Worry less about getting it "right" and concentrate on telling us a story.

13a. Sometimes you start off on the wrong foot. That's okay. You can stop and ask if you can start again. Take a breath. Focus. Start again. If it doesn't happen the second time, you should kindly apologize and leave the room. You're not prepared. You've not done enough work on the piece, or you're letting your nerves get the better of you. There are no tried-and-true tricks for beating this. Comfort and familiarity with the material, combined with a desire to tell the story, are your best bets!

14. Keep it to two minutes. All of the monologues in this book fulfill that requirement, and some are shorter. You do not need to use the entire two minutes. We can very often tell if we're interested in someone within the first thirty seconds to a minute.

15. When you've finished, take a beat and end the piece. Give us a cue that your performance is over and you're no longer the character. Again, be careful of judging your work while in the room. I've seen many actors want to apologize or make a face that says, "Well, that didn't go the way I had planned it." Whether it was your best work or your worst work, don't let us know.

16. There's a fine line between lingering and rushing out of the room. Sometimes we may ask you a question or two in an effort to get to know you better. Stay focused and centered until we say, "Thank you."

17. Your résumé should be a reflection of your work. Please don't lie on it in any way, shape, or form! Don't say you've worked with people or on productions that you never have! If you were in the ensemble, don't say you were the lead! We've all been in the ensemble. It's okay.

18. Enjoy the storytelling.

In this book I'm providing you with a summary of the play, a brief character description, and a list of questions you should ask yourself when approaching the material. However, I urge you to seek out the play and read it in its entirety so that you can have a greater understanding of the character, the situations, and the events.

Most importantly, when performing any of these pieces, play a strong, simple, vivid objective; maintain a deep emotional connection to the material; act on the line; have a sense of urgency; and know why, and to whom, you're speaking.

Some of the monologues included in this volume are very short. I find it's helpful to have these in your back pocket in case you are asked to do something else and want something quick that packs a punch. As I said earlier, you can provide a good sense of what you can do in a relatively short amount of time.

Conversely, some of these pieces are long. I am providing you with alternate cuts within the larger structure that, I believe, maintain the original intent of the author and still provide storytelling opportunities.

Etiquette for Scene Study, Rehearsal, and Beyond

My recent experiences as a college professor and associate director led me to discover that some of the things I assumed were obvious (in regard to behavior, attitude, and work ethic) for actors of all ages and levels were, in fact, not.

The second you walk in the door, you are there to serve the work, not your ego.

No matter who you are in the show, you are part of an ensemble, and every move you make affects that. The ensemble extends to everyone working on the production: stage management, director, crew, stage door man, et cetera. Each of these people deserves your attention and respect.

I compiled this list in response to that discovery and have a feeling it will keep evolving over my lifetime and, hopefully, beyond. It might not necessarily serve you in an audition setting, but keep it in mind once you book the work.

First-Day-of-Rehearsal Behavior
- Be present. Everyone is nervous and excited.
    - Do not isolate yourself.
    - Approach individuals and introduce yourself.
    - Tell them what your role is (even if you're an understudy).
    - Make conversation by asking questions and talking about your résumé.
    - Seek out the director, producer, and casting director and thank them for the opportunity.

- During the read-through, don't highlight your lines. *Listen* to the play.
- During the read-through, don't look ahead to see when you're next on stage. *Listen* to the play.

First Read-through and Every Rehearsal

- Dress appropriately
  - Dress in a silhouette similar to your character's. If your character wears long pants, do not rehearse in shorts. If your character wears a skirt, wear a skirt.
  - Do not wear clothing with logos or slogans printed on it. You want your partner focusing on you, your face, your body, and your behavior, not reading your T-shirt or laughing at the funny print on it.
  - Do not wear open-toed shoes or sandals ever, unless the role requires them. Do not rehearse a fight scene in these shoes ever.
  - Do not change your hair length, color, or style at any time before rehearsal starts or during the process without consulting your director first.
- Practice personal hygiene
  - Brush your teeth before every rehearsal and after every break, especially after eating or smoking.
  - Shower every day and before every performance.
  - Wear clean clothes to rehearsal every day. If you wear the same things, figure out a way to wash them as much as possible.
  - Go to the gym. Eight shows a week require strength and stamina. Film shoots can be long and exhausting.
  - If you go to the gym before rehearsal, shower.
  - Get seven to eight hours of sleep a night.
  - Drink and smoke in moderation.

- Bring a pencil and paper with you. Every day. Have backups.
- Phones are not a place to take notes at any time during the process.
- Character idea: Have one based on an intelligent reading and analysis of the script.
- Your character idea should be flexible. The director may steer you in a different direction. Try it for a few days. If it doesn't feel right, explain this and use your reading and analysis of the script to support your case. Ultimately, your director has the final say.
- Don't emphasize pronouns and verbs. These are very often the least interesting words in the sentence.
- Don't be late. Give yourself time to arrive at least ten minutes early. You should be ready to work at start time, not arriving. If you need time to warm up, factor this into your travel time.
- *Listen.* Listen to everyone.
- Pay attention to what the director says about the world of the play. Even if it does not immediately give you information about your character specifically, he or she is sharing their vision of the show with you. You can very often pick up something valuable to use immediately or in the future as you create your character. This information informs your choices.
- Don't ask too many questions right away. Don't make everything about your character and you. The rehearsal process is one of discovery, and you shouldn't discover everything in the first week. Also, if you *listen*, you may discover the answers to your questions without having to ask.
- Look up the definition and pronunciation of any unfamiliar word or reference.
- Find an activity for every scene you're in. We rarely sit and talk. Activity creates behavior. This activity should be rooted in the text and what the text says you could or should be doing.

- Don't confuse your *fear* with your *process*. It is your job to take risks in rehearsal, and this doesn't always happen in your comfort zone or when you are ready to.
- *Jump* when the director asks you to without asking "How high?" first.
- Don't use the word "process" to defend your insecurities. The director has a process, too, and that's to get a performance out of you, and it doesn't always happen on your terms. Your "process" is not an excuse to not try something the director is asking.
- Unless otherwise instructed, be off-book the second time you get to a scene.
- Use the rehearsal room as your opportunity to *take chances*.
- Don't stand in your own way. Listen to the script and your director, not your ego.
- Don't enter a scene to "have a scene" with your partner. It's your job to keep that person in the room, and vice versa. You're coming in to achieve something, and the other person is either going to help or hinder you. Live truthfully within that knowledge.
- Always find a sense of urgency in your character.
- Always find a sense of humor in your character.

Men's Monologues

Stanton's Garage
Joan Ackermann

RON

Such an unattractive sound—ex, especially for someone soft you've held naked against your body at night for a decade. Like ax.

See, the problem was I never made it to court. For my divorce. I never went. I didn't want to go. I didn't have to go, my lawyer told me, but . . . it was a mistake.

You have to go to events like that. You have to be there. You have to be at your . . . birth. To get the full effect. You have to go to funerals, watch the body being lowered into the ground, being covered with dirt, shovelful by shovelful. Then you know . . . you know where the body is. In the ground. There's no doubt.

You have to go to your own divorce, sit in the courtroom, hold your coat in your lap, look at the judge, look at your lawyer, look at her lawyer. Make the appropriate expressions. Hear the flies. Then you have something. Then you have pieces. Concrete pieces.

I can't see it. I don't have her face getting divorced. I never saw our marriage officially pronounced dead. It's been a problem.

Analysis: *Stanton's Garage*

Type: Dramatic
Synopsis

The action takes place in a small service station in upstate Missouri. It's the only garage for thirty miles.

Silvio, Harlan, and Denny—a motley, well-meaning crew—all work here. Today they're dealing with the broken-down cars of Lee and Ron. Both are on their way to the same wedding, but they don't know it, or each other. The wedding is in the town of St. Joseph. The owner of the garage is in Mexico, so it's very difficult to get a straight answer from anyone about cost, repair specifics, or time. Ron's car gets fixed and he leaves. Harlan, seventeen years old, thinks the problem with Lee's car might be the fuel injectors. When Harlan says he has to drive somewhere to get new injectors, Frannie offers to go with him. Frannie is the sixteen-year-old daughter of Lee's boyfriend. Frannie says she can pick up food on the trip, and she secretly tells Harlan that she'll pierce his ear when they get back.

In actuality, no one at the garage knows how to fix the car. Lee misses the wedding luncheon, then cocktails. Frannie starts pumping gas for customers to kill the time. The staff tells Lee she might need a whole new computer system. After seven hours, Lee finally breaks down and calls Henry, her boyfriend, who is furious with her. He yells at her and hangs up.

Ron appears late at night, with a black eye. Lee, who's sleeping in the garage, thinks it's a burglar and she shoots at him, breaking a $1,000 bottle of wine. Ron says the black eye is from Harry, who was bad-mouthing Lee at the wedding. Ron came to her defense. Morning comes and Lee tells Frannie she's going back to Chicago and leaving Harry. Frannie tells Lee she kissed her first boy, Harlan. The ladies find the Volvo manual, fix the car themselves, and drive home.

Character Description
Ron, 40s

Ron is a wine importer. The thermostat in his car broke on the way to the wedding. He carries a gun in his blazer pocket. He's going to St. Joseph's, uninvited, to his ex-wife's second wedding. Unprovoked, he fires the gun in the garage two times, and then he gives it to Silvio because he doesn't like it. He cuts his hand when banging on a broken gumball machine. He's carrying around a lot of anger, resentment, and fear. While he's waiting for the car to be fixed, his former brother-in-law pulls in for gas but speeds away upon spotting Ron.

He buys forty-eight air fresheners and a box of antifreeze as a wedding present. He accidentally leaves his wallet stuffed with hundred-dollar bills and condoms at the garage. Ron's a guy who can't fix anything. If he knew how to use a screwdriver he'd still be married. His girlfriend has just left him and he doesn't know how to be alone.

Given Circumstances

Who are they? Lee and Ron have briefly met yesterday.

Where are they? Stanton's Garage in upstate Missouri.

When does this take place? The present, 2:00 a.m.

Why are they there? Ron is returning from crashing his ex-wife's wedding.

What is the pre-beat? Lee just asked if his ex's name is Suzanne.

Questions

1. Can you state your objective in a simple, specific, and active way?
2. Who are you talking to? Be specific and have a clear image.
3. Can you think of three adjectives to describe your character?
4. How long were you and Suzanne a couple? Married?
5. How long have you been divorced?

6. Do you still love her?
7. What does she look like?
8. Did she look happy and in love at the wedding?
9. Was the groom handsome? Fit? Is he successful?
10. What does Lee look like?
11. Why did you stand up to Lee's fiancé for her?
12. What do you do for a living?
13. Do you like it?
14. Are you successful?
15. Are you lonely?

Great Falls
Lee Blessing

MONKEY MAN

I was thirteen when I was here before. We went to the hot springs. They didn't have all the stuff they have now, of course.

Mom hated it, said it stank. Which it did, of course. Just . . . overpowering. But even so, Dad and I climbed up to this place above the main spring. It was so beautiful. The water was the clearest I ever . . . well, it had to be, right? What could live in it? And the colors were . . . And all this heat just kind of flowed up from it in big waves, through the air. I could see where humans got their vision of hell, you know? So beautiful and . . . lethal. Strange to be someplace where the earth's so much hotter than everything else. Guess nobody's sleeping in the cold, cold ground around here, eh?

That was a great trip. I liked my parents best on trips. Wish we'd taken more trips with you and your brother. Bet you guys would have traveled well.

Are you asleep?

Analysis: *Great Falls*

Type: Dramatic
Synopsis
Monkey Man and Bitch are in a car in the Great Northwest just driving around. Bitch accuses him of kidnapping her—a twenty-mile ride has turned into two hundred. Monkey Man made Bitch promise

not to call her mom, but a day into the trip she finally breaks down
and does it. From there, the relationship between the two characters
begins to get clearer.

Monkey Man is Bitch's former stepfather. He was married to her
mom. Bitch has given them both these names because he acts like
a monkey and thinks she's a bitch. They're not allowed to use each
other's real names.

Bitch's mom goes off on Monkey Man but doesn't demand he
bring her home. She makes them stop at a drug store so that Bitch
can get everything she needs. He hangs up and Bitch screams at him
that he's not her father. He says they'll get a motel room. He really
needs to talk to her. Bitch says no to a motel and demands they sleep
in the car. After an uncomfortable night in the car, the trip continues
and Bitch relents to a motel for the next evening. They're in the land
of hot springs. He suggests they stay for a day and see the sights. He
buys her cigarettes but books a non-smoking room. Bitch showers
and sleeps almost in the nude. Monkey Man tries to talk to her, but
she falls asleep.

He's taking her to all the sights his parents took him when he
was a kid. He's trying to be a father to Bitch. She finally refuses to
go any farther unless she can drive. Monkey Man relents. He finally
confesses that had so many affairs because he was scared Bitch's
mom would be the last woman he ever had sex with and he wasn't
emotionally ready for the commitment of marriage. He feels terrible
about it and wishes that Bitch and her fourteen-year-old brother
would talk to him again.

Bitch tells him the story of how she lost her virginity to two men,
how they forced her, and now she finds herself pregnant. There's a
Planned Parenthood in Great Falls and she wants Monkey Man to
go with her to get an abortion and pay for it. He owes her for what
he's done to the family. He does. The recovery takes longer than

usual because the doctor finds that she also caught chlamydia from one of the boys.

They end their journey back where they started. Monkey Man gifts Bitch his car. She says she wrote him a haiku right before surgery and asks if he wants to hear it. He tells her to save it as this isn't goodbye.

Character Description
Monkey Man, 40s

When he was ten his parents took him on a trip to this area of the country. They saw it all: Mount Rushmore, Devil's Tower, Pompey's Pillar, et cetera. Is in a relationship with B's mom, but is not her father. Eats bagels. Can't think unless he's driving, or walking, or on the move somehow. Says he'll pay B for the loss of her job. Even though B and her brother aren't his children, he pays child support for them—by choice. Tells B she always acts like she's seven years old around her. Really wants to talk to B, but she won't allow it. Asks if he can call her by her real name. Every day he was with B's mom he was in pain, and the affairs were a kind of instant relief. He realizes it's not the cheating that's the worst, it's the humiliation. Knows he's average. Used to write poetry but doesn't anymore. Now writes fiction. Wishes he had adopted the kids legally when he was married to their mom so he had some rights.

Given Circumstances

Who are they? Bitch is the daughter of Monkey Man's ex.

Where are they? Thermopolis, Wyoming.

When does this take place? The present. Evening.

Why are they there? Monkey Man is taking Bitch on a tour of places he went with his parents as a child.

What is the pre-beat? Bitch looks at his body and says, "I can see why she left you."

Questions

1. Can you state your objective in a simple, specific, and active way?
2. Who are you talking to? Be specific and have a clear image.
3. Can you think of three adjectives to describe your character?
4. Do you feel old?
5. When did your body start to change?
6. Were you in love with Bitch's mother?
7. Do you miss having kids around?
8. What sparked the idea for this tour of Midwest attractions?
9. What does Bitch look like?
10. When was the last time you saw her?
11. How has she changed?
12. Were you close to her when she was a child?
13. Do you feel guilty for leaving her as well as her mom?
14. Were you close with her brother, too?
15. What do you do for a living? How did you manage this time off?

Jericho
Jack Canfora

JOSH

I pushed people out of my way. To get downstairs. After the elevators failed. I pushed past people. Not many, like three, I think, and not, you know, viciously, I didn't knock them down. But only because I didn't have to. They were slow and I didn't want to get caught behind them.

One of them was this heavy set, older woman. Black. The other two were white men—not old men at all, thirties, forties maybe. They . . . were trying to help her. Help move her down the stairs. She was hurt, somehow, not too badly, but . . . she needed help. She was crying and praying. They asked me to—they needed me to help them. Just help them a little bit. I just . . . I shoved right past them. I don't know . . . it's a blur.

These people. Who knows who they are, if they're alive. If they made it. Your husband, for all we'll ever know. I don't even—you'd think something like that—their faces would be burned in my mind, but for the life of me, I can't . . . it's a blur. I've only told one other person about that day. Jessica. She said to me, she pulled me close to her and whispered "Baby as long as you're alive and safe."

I've since realized that was the moment I knew I could never love her again.

Analysis: *Jericho*

Type: Dramatic
Synopsis

Beth, the main character of this family drama, is dealing with the long-term effects of having lost her husband in the September 11, 2001, attack on the World Trade Center. She has been in therapy for a number of years and has just begun dating someone. Overwhelmed by Alec's death, Beth is on antidepressants and she literally sees her forty-seven-year-old Korean American female therapist in her husband's form.

Ethan, Beth's new boyfriend, is anxious for her to let Alec go so that they can move forward—they've been dating three months and have still not had sex—with the relationship. He invites Beth to spend Thanksgiving with his family. Beth, who still spends the holiday with her in-laws, agrees. The big question of the play seems to be: how do you move on without letting go of the past?

Ethan's family is Jewish, and they celebrate at his mom's house in Jericho, Long Island. Josh, Ethan's brother, was also in the World Trade Center on the day of the attacks. He and his wife, Jessica, are in a very tense period of their marriage. Josh wants them to move to Israel. He found religion after the attacks, springing from an extreme case of guilt because he pushed past people while fleeing the building. Jessica wants none of this. She wants her husband back, not this religious fanatic that has taken his place.

The day gets even tenser as secrets are revealed. Josh discovers Beth is partly Palestinian. Ethan reveals to his brother that he's still sleeping with his office's receptionist. Rachel, Josh and Ethan's mother, reveals she wants to sell the family home to Josh and Jessica and move to Florida. Josh and Jessica end their marriage. Every character's state of mind is eloquently summed up by Beth when she says, "I can't stay connected to anyone. Anyone. Or any place. Least of all myself."

Character Description
Josh, 40s
Josh is married to Jessica. They are having major marital problems. He watches TV news constantly. He oftentimes corrects her grammar, driving her crazy. He doesn't like to answer the phone. He turns the sound down on the answering machine so he doesn't have to hear the messages. He observes the Jewish faith. He wants to move to Israel—Jessica does not. He thinks everyone in America has their heads up their asses. He found his religion after 9/11. He stopped loving Jessica when she comforted him after he confessed his 9/11 behavior by saying, "Baby, as long as you're safe."

Given Circumstances
Who are they? Josh is talking to Beth, his brother's girlfriend.
Where are they? The living room of Josh's mother's Long Island home.
When does this take place? 2005.
Why are they there? It's Thanksgiving Day.
What is the pre-beat? Beth tells Josh losing her husband on 9/11 is none of his business.

Questions
1. Can you state your objective in a simple, specific, and active way?
2. Who are you talking to? Be specific and have a clear image.
3. Can you think of three adjectives to describe your character?
4. How long have you and Jessica been married?
5. What does she look like?
6. Where in your body do you feel her when you think about her?

7. Where do you feel the weight of 9/11 in your body?
8. How often during the day do you think about this event?
9. What does your faith do for you?
10. Why do you want Jessica to participate in religion with you?
11. What does Israel mean to you?
12. What kind of life do you want to have there?
13. Are you really willing to sacrifice your entire life to move there?
14. Who is Beth?
15. What do you see when you look at her?

The Day I Stood Still
Kevin Elyot

HORACE

It's so nice seeing you without a lump on your head — God, I'm sorry!

You used to have one as a baby (*indicating the middle of the forehead*). You didn't know, did you?

God, I am sorry. Jerry thought you were from another planet. He said it was an implanted radio to receive messages from your mother ship.

It went, apparently, of its own accord. It seems these things come and go. I didn't mean to . . . I'm sorry.

That was the last time I saw Jerry. Your christening, which was the first time I saw you.

We had a great time, your dad and me. Not at the christening. Well, it was alright, as christenings go — not that I've been to many — any, really — oh, well, one or two. But when we were younger — your dad — your dad was everything that was — happy and good then — at that time in my life, and which has gone now — like him.

There was one day, one day we had — when I met your mother, actually — which was sort of complete. One of those moments in life when you realize, 'Ah, that's what it's like to be happy.' I hoped there'd be more days like that, but there weren't. Not quite like that, anyway. When I'm dying, it's that moment that'll make me think it was all worthwhile. My life crystallized in the memory of a moment. It was like we were outside time.

A moment? It's not a minute or a second. It's a mystery. A moment is a part of the mystery of life.

Analysis: *The Day I Stood Still*

Type: Dramatic
Synopsis

Judy shows up unexpectedly on Horace's North London doorstep. They haven't seen each other in four years. Horace was best friends with Judy's husband, Jerry. Horace was, in fact, in love with Jerry. Once Jerry and Judy married, they saw Horace less and less frequently. Jerry died unexpectedly of blood poisoning when he cut himself on a piece of metal binding, reading Horace's manuscript.

Judy has arrived with her new French boyfriend, Guy. She has left her young son, Jimi, with his nanny. Horace is awaiting the arrival of a rent boy. Judy keeps calling the nanny to check on her son and finds out that he's missing. She and Guy run back to their hotel. Horace finds himself opening up to the rent boy but unable to sleep with him. They have an intense conversation and then Horace is left alone.

The second scene jumps forward in time some twelve years. Jimi, now a young man, appears at Horace's door. He's run away from boarding school. Jimi is here because Horace knew his father. Jimi had a dream the night before and his father appeared to him. Jimi wanted to come here and find out more about Jerry. And so, Horace tells him about his Jerry. As the two men get drunk and high, Horace tells Jimi he used to have a chain of his father's but lost it a long time ago. Jimi's foot goes through a floorboard uncovering the chain and closing the scene.

The final scene of the play flashes back thirty years to when Horace, Jerry, and Judy were seventeen. It's the last perfect day that Horace can remember.

Character Description
Horace, 40s

Horace works at a museum. He's a writer, tried to get a novel published once. He "sometimes wonders how many ideas a person has in a lifetime—good ones . . . One or two, if you're lucky." He's the godfather of Jimi, whom he only saw once at the christening. He likes children from when they're about fifteen years on. He listens to Beethoven. He doesn't really know where he's going in life.

Given Circumstances
Who are they? Horace is Jimi's godfather but hasn't seen him since the christening.
Where are they? Horace's apartment.
When does this take place? The late 1990s.
Why are they there? Jimi has run away from boarding school.
What is the pre-beat? Jimi has just offered Horace cocaine.

Questions
1. Can you state your objective in a simple, specific, and active way?
2. Who are you talking to? Be specific and have a clear image.
3. Can you think of three adjectives to describe your character?
4. What do you write about?
5. Do you write every day? For how long?
6. How do you support yourself?
7. What was your first novel about?
8. Do you feel responsible for Jerry's death?
9. How often do you hire rent boys?
10. When is the last time you went out socially?
11. What does seeing Jimi make you feel?
12. What does seeing Jimi make you want?

13. Does Jimi look like Jerry?

14. Did you ever want a family?

15. How does your apartment make you feel?

Middletown
Will Eno

MECHANIC

I was nervous, earlier. I don't know why. Well, I do know—for part of it, I was being choked. And I'm nervous now, now that I think of it. But I'm nothing special, postnatally speaking. I fix cars, I try to. I get hassled by the cops, try to maintain a certain—I don't know—sobriety.

Sometimes, I volunteer at the hospital, dress up for the kids. It was part of a plea deal. But what isn't. Nothing really crazy to report.

Except, I found this rock once, everyone. What I thought was a meteorite. I brought the thing into the school, here. The kids ran it through all these tests, tapped on it, shined lights at it. I found it in a field. It looked special.

Then the astronaut here told me it was just a rock. Said it was probably from, at some earlier time, another slightly larger rock. His name is Greg Something. I had ideas about getting famous, getting on local TV with my meteorite. When it turned out to be just a rock, I thought I could still make some headlines with it if I threw it off a bridge, hit some family in their car and killed everybody. But then I figured, you know what, forget it, that's not me. So now some family's driving around, not knowing how lucky they are, not knowing how sweet it all is. Just because.

Analysis: *Middletown*

Type: Seriocomic
Synopsis and Character Description

"Middletown. Population: stable; elevation: same. The main street is called Main Street. The side streets are named after trees. Things are fairly predictable. People come, people go. Crying, by the way, in both directions."

Middletown is exactly what it sounds like: an average American small town. Will Eno's play is kind of modern day *Our Town*. It's a meditation on the beauty and mystery of life. Each character is, in their own way, trying to navigate the tricky pathways of life, love, and interpersonal relationships. Everyone is trying to find out the meaning of their lives.

The Mechanic is in his forties. He's one of the town's lost souls. When we first meet him he's sitting in a park drinking alcohol concealed in a paper bag. He tosses some trash onto the ground and gets into a confrontation with the town cop. The confrontation ends with the cop choking Mechanic with his baton for a good few seconds.

At the heart of the story is the blossoming love affair between Mary Swanson, a pregnant woman recently moved to town, and John Dodge, the local plumber. Mary's husband is often away on business.

In a scene with the librarian, she recalls how the Mechanic wrote an essay when he was a child titled, "This Whole Hamlet Is Shaking." She had it hanging in the library for years and he had his picture in the paper. He recalls how he was shaking when he read the essay and muses that someone probably scared his mother before he was born and she gave him "shaky blood."

The story of Middletown is told in a series of vignettes that ultimately reveal the loneliness and longing that all the characters share and only the few who can actually make a connection.

Given Circumstances

Who are they? Mechanic, born and raised in Middletown, USA.

Where are they? Technically, he's in the town's library.

When does this take place? The present.

Why are they there? He's just passing through.

What is the pre-beat? He overhears the Librarian and Mary Swanson talking about prenatal books.

Questions

1. Can you state your objective in a simple, specific, and active way?
2. Who are you talking to? Be specific and have a clear image.
3. Can you think of three adjectives to describe your character?
4. What town is comparable to Middletown for you, a sort of "Anytown, USA"?
5. How many times have you left town in your lifetime?
6. How much do you drink?
7. What does drinking make you feel?
8. Is alcohol the only reason you get hassled by the cops?
9. Who are your friends in town?
10. When and why did you make the decision to become a mechanic?
11. What does your job mean to you?
12. How does your job define you?
13. Are you lonely?
14. What does overhearing this talk of marriage and babies make you feel?
15. How often do you come to the library? Are you a reader?

The Hologram Theory
Jessica Goldberg

SIMON

Do you know what a hologram is?

Say I have a photograph of me and you sitting here in this very restaurant.

Now, say I take the photograph and rip it up into fifty small pieces and throw them on the table. When I pick up a piece I'll have your eye, you have lovely eyes, or your lips, you have beautiful lips—

And as much as I'd like to have just your lips or eyes . . . what good are your lips without mine, your eyes without mine?

If I have a hologram of me and you sitting here in this very restaurant and I rip that up into fifty small pieces and throw them on the table, when I pick a piece up, I will have the whole picture of you and I sitting here in the very restaurant. You see, in a hologram, a true hologram, every piece contains the whole. We are all pieces of the whole, Sara. In this world, this life, my stories are your stories, yours are mine. We are all a part of the whole. So, I feel no guilt.

I'm beginning to have deviant thoughts about you. I like how your face turned red when I said the word "sex." Oh, there it goes again.

If I take you to my favorite room at the Gramercy Park Hotel you must promise not to add that to your interview.

I'm an artist. It's our job, to penetrate.

Analysis: *The Hologram Theory*

Type: Dramatic
Synopsis and Character Description

Simon Spence, in his forties, is the father of Julian. Simon is a successful, elite film director. Julian is a club kid.

Patsy, a Trinidadian artist, is haunted by visions of her twin brother, Dominic. Dominic tells her he's dead and she needs to come to NYC to find out what happened to him and put him to rest.

In a series of short, clipped scenes, like fragments of a hologram, Goldberg unravels the story of drug abuse, partying, excess, and murder. The story is tied together by the character of Sara, a journalist looking to land her first big story. Sara's sister Mimi points her in the right direction when she admits her friends killed a drug dealer and cut up his body.

The first time we see Simon and Julian together they are eating in silence at a fancy restaurant. Simon doesn't like that Julian lies. He doesn't like that Julian apologizes for everything. Simon explains that when he was Julian's age he worked four jobs, put himself through school, and took care of his mother. Simon was motivated and wanted to live his life, so it's shocking to him that Julian is his son, as he seemingly has no ambition. And Simon never apologized for anything.

Simon is getting ready to leave town for a while. He hired a house sitter and doesn't want Julian going over there. Julian is his mother's responsibility since she's the one that raised him. Simon gives Julian a substantial check to hold him over for the few months that he'll be in Cannes.

Julian explains that his mom won't let him stay with her because she thinks he's a drug addict. Simon says he is. Simon says he looks at Julian and tries to understand how this happened, where he went wrong. And could it go wrong with his new children? Simon doesn't recognize Julian anymore.

Simon came to NYC from his hometown of Huntsville and fought to be someone, if only to make everyone who rejected him take notice. He has three children with his new wife and an "unconventional marriage."

Julian calls Simon for help, admitting that he murdered someone. Simon tries to get him out of his circle of friends, cover this up, and clean him up. Julian can't resist the pull of his friends, though. Only when he meets Patsy does he realize the enormity of what he did and turn himself in to the police.

Given Circumstances

Who are they? Sara is a reporter. The two have just met.

Where are they? A bar on the Upper East Side of Manhattan.

When does this take place? The present.

Why are they there? Sara has arranged an interview.

What is the pre-beat? Sara has just asked Simon if he ever feels guilty putting so much of his real life into his films.

Questions

1. Can you state your objective in a simple, specific, and active way?
2. Who are you talking to? Be specific and have a clear image.
3. Can you think of three adjectives to describe your character?
4. What is Sara's most attractive feature?
5. At what moment did you decide to sleep with her?
6. How close to her are you sitting?
7. Is this an expensive bar?
8. How crowded is it?
9. How would you describe your films?

10. What drives you to tell stories in this medium?
11. Are you proud of the work you've accomplished?
12. How would you describe your relationship to your ex-wife?
13. How would you describe your relationship to your current wife?
14. How open is your relationship, and how often do you take advantage of that?
15. Where would you rank "father" on your list of accomplishments?

Victory Jones
Idris Goodwin

JAMES

Evening.

Um

This don't look like much of a hip hop crowd but uhm, I used to make rap music.

For a while.

My daughter is here.

She's trying to do her music thing too.

I call myself teaching her the essential lessons.

When she told me she wanted to do music I asked her "Why" which seems like a simple question but can sometimes be a little tough to answer.

My own father asked me that question. "Why?"

See I was real shy, real quiet when I was a kid.

But when I started rapping I found that I could say whatever I needed to.

And still, now, sometimes it's easier to tell the truth in rhyme form.

Deep breath

TURN ON THE TV
WHAT DO I SEE
NEW SCHOOL RAPPERS
TRYIN TO BE LIKE ME

THEY GOT BLING
THEY GOT WHIPS
THEY GOT LADIES

BUT CAN THEY HOLD IT DOWN ON THE MIC?

I BROUGHT RAP INTO THE HOMES OF
MILLIONS
BACK WHEN WHITE FOLKS KEPT RAP
FROM THEY CHILDREN

AND FOLKS WANNA KNOW
WHY YOU QUIT THAT RAP?
THE MONEY? THE FAME?
WHY YOU GO AND DO THAT?

YOU WAS VICTORY DANCIN'
UP AT THE GRAMMYS
DID YOU LEAVE IT ALL BEHIND
TO GO RAISE UP A FAMILY?

YOU HAD A HIT
HAD A WHIP
HAD A LADY
WAS IT BECAUSE SHE WENT AND HAD A
BABY?

(pause)

Sorry—
Yeah uhm I still need another verse.

Analysis: *Victory Jones*

Type: Dramatic
Synopsis

The play opens with April showing up at her dad's front door in Albuquerque, New Mexico. She's just graduated from college in Chicago. April calls her father "Victory." Their relationship is stiff and formal. Victory congratulates her on her graduation, and it's obvious that this is the first time he's acknowledged the event. April's mom told her that Victory was out of work. He avoids this particular conversation by making pancakes.

April has her looping station with her. She uses it to create her music. She explains to Victory how it works. It's her instrument. Victory doesn't understand it at all. The power goes out while April shows him how the instrument works. Victory hasn't paid the electric bill in full. April plays a full song for him on her phone and he's truly impressed. She then informs him that his Grammy performance is back in the Zeitgeist. April wants him to help her make an album. He's her one industry connection. Victory is cautious but relents.

Victory takes April to an open-mic night at a club so that he can see her perform. April resists, and Victory makes it clear she's now enrolled in his academy. April's set isn't very successful, but Joe, the host, takes an interest in her. Victory finds out April is pregnant. She doesn't want to talk about the baby or return the father's calls/text messages.

Joe also becomes a teacher to April. Together they school her on not only music, but also the industry and how it functions. Joe runs an open mic for teenagers, and he brings Victory and April with him to help. April gets angry and storms out.

Goodwin is exploring the old versus the new using rap and technology as his foundation. April thinks she doesn't have to play by the old rules, that she can create a new road to success, and Victory is proving her wrong step by step. The tension between them is only heightened by the fact that he was an absentee father for most of her life.

Joe and April seem interested in each other, romantically. Joe talks to Victory about her. He tells Victory he needs to let April know she has serious potential. He also says he might be moving to Chicago. Victory tells him he needs to slow down.

April thinks Victory quit because her mom got pregnant. He takes her to another open mic and performs the above rap, and then reveals that the label liked his look and sound but not his voice, so they hired someone to dub him. Once he started lip-syncing the label wouldn't let him sing live again. So, Victory quit.

Ultimately Victory, April, and Joe become a team and create music together,

Character Description
James "Victory" Jones, 42

James was once an energetic and creative rapper from Chicago. These days he's a bit more sullen and detached. He's an unemployed high school teacher and basketball coach who hasn't picked up a mic in a long time. His daughter, April, is twenty-one years old and a musician. April says he hasn't seen her since she was "sixteen and depressed." Victory says it hasn't been that long, but it's been a while. He tells April not to call him "Victory" but doesn't like "Dad" either. He doesn't have a cell phone. He has very little money and no income. He doesn't listen to any music produced past 1994. Victory prays before eating. He used to be really famous, performed "Victory Dance" on the Grammys telecast in the 1990s, and now everyone's watching it on YouTube. He says rappers aren't musicians. He decided to be a rapper instead of going to college. He had planned on moving to Las Cruces, New Mexico, but uses his final unemployment check to help April.

Given Circumstances

Who are they? Victory is performing in front of bikers and his daughter.

Where are they? A biker bar in Madrid, New Mexico.

When does this take place? The present.

Why are they there? Victory is trying to teach his daughter about the music business.

What is the pre-beat? Andrea, the bar manager, announces there's $78 in the hat for tonight's winner and then calls Victory to the stage.

Questions

1. Can you state your objective in a simple, specific, and active way?
2. Who are you talking to? Be specific and have a clear image.
3. Can you think of three adjectives to describe your character?
4. Do you miss making music?
5. Have you been creating it in your head all these years? Writing any of it down?
6. What do you love about performing?
7. Do you miss your family?
8. Why did your marriage fail?
9. What kind of father have you been?
10. When was the last time you did any kind of work?
11. Where did your ambition go?
12. Were you happy to see April when she showed up at your door?
13. How does it feel educating your daughter about the business?
14. Does April look like your ex-wife? Does she look like you?
15. When is the last time you performed in front of an audience?

Death Tax
Lucas Hnath

TODD

I think you think I'm weak.
I think you're used to the type of guys
who push people around
and I'm not that type of person.

But I think I bore you.
I think you miss the other type of guy.
I think you don't want to be with someone like me.
I think I embarrass you.
You'd rather be with someone who, I dunno,
who wore leather jackets.

Yeah, you know what I mean
Leather jackets.
Rides a motorcycle.
I have cardigans. Polo shirts.
Khaki pants.

The time when we went out and had dinner,
and I saw you looking at the guy at the bar wearing a leather
    jacket,
I saw you looking at him,
and I could see you seeing in your eye
that you'd rather be with him.
And that was just a week before we decided to take a break.

That was just a week before, but when I saw you seeing him,
in his leather jacket, I could tell you were
And I wish I were that person.
I wish I were a leather jacket guy, Tina.
I try.
I want to be that guy.
I think that's why I want to be with you, I think,
I think, because I think that being with you
would help maybe make me more the type of guy that I want
     to be.
But you just don't have patience for me I guess.

Analysis: *Death Tax*

Type: Dramatic
Synopsis

The action of the play takes place in a nursing home in December 2010. Maxine, an elderly woman, near death and very wealthy, is a patient. Tina, a Haitian nurse, takes care of her. One day during a routine vitals check Maxine says to Tina, "I know that you are killing me." Tina denies this accusation.

Maxine has her shut and lock the door. Maxine explains that the tax laws are changing on the first of January. At that point the amount of money her daughter will receive upon Maxine's death with decrease substantially. Maxine believes that her daughter, knowing Tina makes very little money, offered her an incentive to speed-up her death.

Maxine says her daughter has already asked for, demanded the money, before Maxine's death. Maxine explains she can't change her will at this point.

Maxine knows that Tina has a child in Haiti whom she would like to bring to America. Obviously Tina's job, income, security and well-being are all at stake with this accusation.

Tina finally says that the daughter is going to pay her $1,000 to kill Maxine and another $1,000 when it's done. We don't know if Tina is telling the truth or just trying to get through the situation. Maxine offers her $1,000 for every week she stays alive. If Maxine makes it to January 1 she'll give Tina an additional $200,000.

Tina goes to Todd's office and asks for a leave of absence. Now that she has money she needs to quickly work with lawyers to get her son here. Todd and Tina were lovers. He tells her that another nurse (Nurse Toad) has seen her taking a check from Maxine. This is against policy. Tina points out that this nurse has made false accusations before and they are documented. Tina tells Todd about her deal with Maxine. If Todd can help keep Maxine alive until January 1, then Tina will split the money with him.

Maxine's daughter shows up, but Maxine won't see her. We learn that the daughter is on food stamps and has a young son. She desperately needs money now, but her mother won't even see her. The daughter knows, from Maxine's lawyer, that checks are being written every week—sizable checks—and to whom the money is going. The daughter has had a document drawn up saying she will give up all rights to Maxine's money if she can just see her. She asks Tina to give the papers to Maxine. Todd tells Tina she can't get involved and everything has to stay the way it is.

The action jumps twenty years into the future and Maxine is still alive. She is running out of money and the home is discharging her, but she has nowhere to go and few options. Charley, her grandson, comes but refuses to take her in or pay for her health care. He is mad at Maxine for the way she treated his mother, her daughter. He leaves, and Maxine is left to face her future, her death, alone.

Character Description
Todd Kapinsky, 40s

Todd is a nurse supervisor at the nursing home. Todd and Tina were formerly lovers. Todd is still interested in her. He still tries to protect Tina from things like Nurse Toad's allegations. He wants her to do what's best. He tries to maintain the policies of the home. He has a photo of Tina accepting a check from Maxine. He attempts to give Tina every way out of the situation. Todd has offered Tina money before to help out. She refused it. He's offered to let her move in with him rent-free. He thinks they are only on a break, not broken up.

Given Circumstances

Who are they? Todd is Tina's boss and sometimes lover.
Where are they? Todd's office in the hospital.
When does this take place? December 2010.
Why are they there? Tina has come to ask for a leave of absence.
What is the pre-beat? Todd confesses that he really likes Tina.

Questions

1. Can you state your objective in a simple, specific, and active way?
2. Who are you talking to? Be specific and have a clear image.
3. Can you think of three adjectives to describe your character?
4. What do you find most attractive about Tina?
5. How long ago did the two of you start seeing each other?
6. Who initiated the relationship?
7. Have you ever dated an employee before?
8. What do your duties as "nurse supervisor" entail?

9. What are your suspicions about Tina's leave of absence?
10. What do you think about this money exchange between Tina and Maxine?
11. Who is Nurse Toad?
12. If she's a known/documented liar, why do you believe Nurse Toad now?
13. How much money do you make a year?
14. Can you actually spare money to loan Tina?
15. Do you see yourself as weak, or strong?

While You Lie
Sam Holcroft

CHRIS

I've missed your smell. I've been craving to touch you all day.

What's wrong? Don't you want to? I think about you all the time. I don't know what you've done to me. I've never fucked a foreigner before. This feels so . . . exotic.

I'll lock the door.

Look. Today I was in my car and a woman stopped by my window on her bicycle. She was powerfully muscular, okay? And as the lights changed she powered down on the pedals, the muscles went tight beneath the skin and she took off. And it was . . .

(*He tries to find the words for the sexuality of it.*)

It was . . .

It is about weighing up the risk. Even the women I do not fuck are an assessment of risk.

Yes. You are worth the risk.

Analysis: *While You Lie*

Type: Seriocomic
Synopsis

The plays begins in the bedroom of Ana and Edward. They are forty minutes late for a party, but Ana is still undecided about what to wear. The two fight. Edward says, "I long to be honest with you but you're so sensitive that I have to watch everything I say." Ana says the relationship is over and kicks him out. Ana is very insecure. She lives in England, but she is a foreigner. She wants to be successful but lacks the confidence in herself necessary to succeed.

In the next scene we see Ana at work, wearing Edward's shirt. Chris is her boss and Ana, his secretary. She's demanding a raise and suggests that sex might be in the cards if he obliges. Meanwhile Chris has a child and a pregnant wife, Helen, at home.

Ana goes home and packs up Edward's things. He comes to collect them and they have yet another argument, this one about Ana sleeping with Chris. Edward goes to Chris's home—he had been there at a barbecue the previous summer—to confront Chris. Helen is home alone and Edward finds himself unable to do it. He makes a sexual advance on Helen and she rejects him.

As Ana and Chris's affair escalates, Helen begins to suspect something. She goes to a plastic surgeon to research several surgical options that will keep her looking young, fit, and beautiful. She plans on paying for this with the money Chris gave her to remodel the kitchen.

Amy, Helen and Chris's five-year-old daughter, begins acting up at school. Helen feels the pressure of solo parenting coupled with Chris's affair pulling her apart.

While You Lie is a brilliant dissection of two relationships and how one action can affect many people. Holcroft also shows our ability to be one thing with someone and then totally different with another. He explores the various forms of humiliation we go through put others through, both willingly and unknowingly. Holcroft also demonstrates how far someone will go to be seen in their relationship.

Character Description
Chris, early 40s
Chris is married to Helen, has a baby on the way, and has a five-year-old daughter named Amy. Ana is his assistant and in her early

twenties. While she aspires to something greater, he has her make coffee for him, pick out presents for his wife, and fetch his laundry. He knowingly puts off a conversation about Ana's raise until she brings up the possibility of sex. They have sex in the office and in cheap hotel rooms. Chris and Helen have a large, well-kept, expensive home. Whenever Helen comes close to calling him out on his bad behavior or demanding an explanation, Chris promises her something (like redecorating the kitchen) to cut her off. Ana begins to make more workplace demands, so Chris demands more from her sexually.

Given Circumstances
Who are they? Ana is Chris's secretary.
Where are they? Chris's office.
When does this take place? The present.
Why are they there? It is a workday.
What is the pre-beat? Ana is looking at pictures of women who've been disfigured.

Questions
1. Can you state your objective in a simple, specific, and active way?
2. Who are you talking to? Be specific and have a clear image.
3. Can you think of three adjectives to describe your character?
4. What is Ana's most attractive feature?
5. How long has your affair with her been going on?
6. Had you thought about sleeping with her before that?
7. What business are you in?
8. Do you consider yourself successful?
9. Would you consider yourself happily married?
10. How long have you and Helen been married?

11. Are you still attracted to her?

12. Are you looking forward to having another child?

13. Do you want the baby to be a boy, or a girl?

14. How would you define "family"?

15. What's the urgency behind this monologue?

Strike-Slip
Naomi Iizuka

RICHMOND

You're late. You're always late.

You know this place? It used to be a Japanese restaurant. I used to come in here all the time and have the teriyaki bowl. Now it's—I don't know what the hell it is—Vietnamese, I think. Things change. (*Beat.*) How long has it been, Vince? Has it been a year? Man o man, time flies. I just retired. I don't think you knew that.

It's a new day. All that bullshit I used to have to deal with, guys jamming you up cause they can, saying shit about you soon as you turn your back, never giving you the respect you deserve. I'm done. It's somebody else's problem now. (*Beat.*) I never did get a chance to thank you. Without you flipping like you did on all your old buddies, I would never have made that last bust. Got a little bronze-plated medal. Got my picture taken with the mayor. Twenty-five years on the force and that's what I get. A handshake and a smile.

Analysis: *Strike-Slip*

Type: Dramatic
Synopsis

A strike-slip is a fault rupture in which pieces of ground move parallel to each other, causing vibrations or shaking.

The play opens in a small market in downtown Los Angeles. Richmond has come in to buy some smokes and lottery tickets. Lee, the Korean owner, gives Richmond change. Richmond says he paid with a ten and a five. Lee says it was a ten and one. The two argue and Richmond leaves with a threatening, "I'll be back."

Lee is the father of Angie. Richmond appears to be plotting something with Vince, to take revenge on Lee. Rafael's mother, Viviana, is a real estate agent and she's about to sell a very expensive home to a Caucasian couple, Dan and Rachel, in Santa Monica. Iizuka slowly unfolds a world in which race, status, and finances dictate how people experience the American Dream.

No one is happy in this world. Viviane wants her son to grow up and be a successful businessman, unlike his father. Dan is having an affair with Vince. Richmond feels oppressed and disrespected.

Angie tries to steal money from her father's store to leave town, and he finds her. He slaps her repeatedly. Vince comes in and offers her money. She refuses him. Viviana finds Rafael packing his gun. She tells him if he takes it to never come back. Someone comes into the market and Lee shoots. Lee ends up in prison for shooting and killing someone.

Vince is in business with Richmond and has been skimming merchandise off the top for himself. Richmond knows this.

Rafael and Angie move in together. She is pregnant. Richmond ropes Rafael into his business. Rachel hits Angie in a car accident. Everyone is connected one way or another, our every move has an effect.

Character Description
Richmond, 40s
Richmond is African American. He smokes Marlboro Lights and buys them by the box. He plays the lottery. Richmond is a threatening presence. He's a man who know what he wants and demands respect. He's a former police officer. He drives a Pontiac GTO. Richmond runs some kind of underground business and it reaches far and wide.

Given Circumstances

Who are they? Vince is criminal who runs an underground ring for Richmond.

Where are they? A downtown L.A. Vietnamese fast food restaurant.

When does this take place? The present.

Why are they there? Some of Richmond's last shipment went missing.

What is the pre-beat? This is the top of the scene.

Questions

1. Can you state your objective in a simple, specific, and active way?
2. Who are you talking to? Be specific and have a clear image.
3. Can you think of three adjectives to describe your character?
4. How long have you known Vince?
5. In the past, you saved Vince from doing federal time: how and why?
6. How long has Vince been working for you?
7. How did you approach Vince initially to get him to work for you?
8. What is your underground business?
9. How did you get involved in it?
10. Do you miss being a cop?
11. What was your favorite part of being a cop?
12. What did you expect on your retirement?
13. Were you running your business before you retired?
14. Do you wish you had gotten married and had children?
15. What about L.A. drives you?

The Veri**on Play
Lisa Kron

LARS

Oh god. Okay. Uh . . . I get so flustered!

Okay, so . . . I'm Lars . . .

Okay . . .

The incident that brought me here was with a credit card company.

Wow, I can't believe this is always so hard.

My um . . . my *boyfriend*

(*Deep sigh.*)

is not very good with money, to say the least. He had some debt, and an offer came in the mail. A credit card that was offering a cash advance at 4% interest.

"That's a good rate," Alex said. He said, "Honey, you're always telling me I'm paying too much interest." And it's true. I was. I was always telling him that.

I said, "Alex, I just don't trust these mail offers," and he said, "Why are you always undermining me?" And I guess, I don't know, I guess I was afraid he was right, because I said, "Okay, Alex, I'll check it out." And I called the company and I was on the phone with a representative for at least 45 minutes going over every line of fine print and it seemed like Alex was right, it was a good deal, and as the call was ending, just to confirm, I said, "Just to confirm, we are talking about a 4% interest rate." And the man said, he said, "Yes, sir, you're all set at 32%." And he hung up the phone.

Well, according to the Supreme Court's 1978 decision, Marquette vs. Omaha Services, it is legal.

I called him right back and said cancel, cancel, cancel, cancel. And he said, "Don't worry. The loan can't go through until you sign the papers so don't sign them and you'll be fine." There were no papers. They just deposited the money into our account.

I called them and said, "We didn't agree to the terms." They said we did.

(*Quietly, ashamed.*)

Not only is my credit rating destroyed. But every day I have to come home to that . . . *Bowflex machine.*

Analysis: *The Veri**on Play*

Type: Comedic
Synopsis

Jenni, a smart, hip, young aspiring professional, finds herself falling down the rabbit hole of billing nightmare with a phone company called Ferizon. In this epically funny play, Lisa Kron dissects not only the dangers of customer service, but the cost of keeping up with trends and the power of technology in today's culture.

A misplaced payment of $153.64 takes over ten months to get processed correctly. Once Jenni tells her story, everyone she meets shares an equivalent (or worse!) tale of customer service woe. Numerous calls to Ferizon, which we see acted out, result in nothing. Jenni finally thinks the situation has been taken care of until one day she receives a call from Ferizon telling her she has an outstanding balance. Jenni comes close to having a breakdown.

She attends a support meeting for a group called PHBICS or "People Hurt Badly By Inadequate Customer Service." It's there that she hears the stories of Lars and Carol and realizes she is not alone. The group meets in a shabby, nondescript East Village tenement building. The meetings are high-stakes and stressful, and result in arguments. It's actually the opposite of what a support group should be.

Jenni receives a call from Ferizon telling her that her service will be cut off for lack of payment. It is. Jenni has a breakdown. She can't go on. She swears she will live without phone service. Some people from PHBICS take her to the Port Authority to show her what waits out there in the rest of the world—worse customer service.

The play ends with an anti-Ferizon musical number. Jenni's phone service gets restored—only to relay to her that she must call Ferizon customer service. We can't escape them. There's no way out. They run the world.

Character Description
Lars, 40s
Lars is a well-meaning gay guy and a bit of a caretaker. Lars wants everyone to be happy. He's often over-accommodating. He'd do anything to help a friend or loved one. He's not above sacrificing his own happiness for the comfort of others.

Given Circumstances
Who are they? A meeting of PHBICS.
Where are they? An ungentrified East Village apartment building.
When does this take place? The present.
Why are they there? It's a support group.
What is the pre-beat? Everyone is sharing their stories so Jenni has a sense of the group.

Questions

1. Can you state your objective in a simple, specific, and active way?
2. Who are you talking to? Be specific and have a clear image.
3. Can you think of three adjectives to describe your character?
4. What exactly flusters you about sharing your story?
5. Do you want to help Jenni?
6. How long have you been in the group?
7. How often do you all meet?
8. What do these meetings do for you?
9. How long have you and Alex been a couple?
10. What does Alex look like?
11. Does he have a job?
12. Does he use the Bowflex machine?
13. What does he do for a living?
14. What do you do for a living?
15. Does sharing this story do anything for you?

The Method Gun
Kirk Lynn and Rude Mechs

ROBERT

You know, what I think's wrong—
The gods—they're tired of us
They think our stories are boring.
They think our theater stinks.
It really gets to you after a while.

And actors are freaks, you know?
You spend all your time with a bunch of actors
and before you know it, you're a freak yourself.
Can't avoid it.

I got a tattoo, see?

(ROBERT *shows off his tattoo. The audience's reaction is discouraging.*)

Looks stupid, doesn't it?
That's it. I'm getting to be a freak, too.
I'm not a complete idiot, yet,
I can still use my head, but my heart . . .
I don't have any passion for anything anymore.
I don't want anything.
I don't need anything.
I don't love anybody—
No, that's not right.
I do love you, Stella Burden.

She found me and gave me work
and now the work I get is based on that work.

Analysis: *The Method Gun*

Type: Seriocomic
Synopsis

The Stella Burden Company's production of Tennessee Williams's
A Streetcar Named Desire has been in rehearsal for nine years. Stella
"left" her company (and students) on August 26, 1972. Stella was a
revered teacher, director, and force in the American theater throughout
the 1960s and 1970s. She walked out on her company, immigrating
to South America, never to be heard from again and giving no reason
for her departure.

For nine years her company of actors have been rehearsing
Streetcar, but without the characters of Stanley, Stella, Mitch, and
Blanche—the main characters. All the students have are "artifacts"
left behind by Stella, including a gun that was loaded promptly upon
her departure but never fired. Stella always kept a loaded gun in the
rehearsal room to "remind us that we can kill each other, or her, or
ourselves, I guess."

Throughout the course of the play, the company demonstrates
some of the Burden training technique such as "Crying Practice,"
during which they must cry for three minutes straight.

During the play, which is really more about relationships than
events, the actors perform exercises, recreate scenes from the nine-
year rehearsal process, and show us scenes from before Stella's
departure. They reveal that Stella had devised this *Streetcar* as a way
of teaching them how to play small roles. One student theorizes that
she left because none of them learned a single thing she was trying
to impart.

Character Description
Robert, 40s

His full name is Robert "Hop" Gilbert. He's been rehearsing the role of Steve in *Streetcar* for the past nine years. Perhaps he has a romantic interest in Elizabeth, his classmate. He holds her when she needs comfort. He earns money by teaching fight choreography workshops to college students. He's been known to show up to rehearsal drunk. He has nerves over performing. He once hit another actor in the face during a scene. He thinks there shouldn't be any more books on theater for at least ten years so that people have time to catch up.

Given Circumstances

Who are they? Carl Reyholt is interviewing Robert about Stella Burden.

Where are they? A theater and rehearsal space.

When does this take place? This particular piece takes place in May 1975.

Why are they there? It's two months before the opening of *Streetcar*.

What is the pre-beat? This monologue is the entire scene.

Questions

1. Can you state your objective in a simple, specific, and active way?
2. Who are you talking to? Be specific and have a clear image.
3. Can you think of three adjectives to describe your character?
4. Who is Carl, and what is your relationship to him?
5. How does it make you feel to give your opinion about theater?
6. What did you learn from Stella?
7. What is your theory on where Stella went?
8. What is the tattoo, and why did you get it?

9. What do you love most about acting?

10. What do you hate most about acting?

11. How do you support yourself?

12. What character do you feel closest to in *Streetcar*?

13. Does it bother you that you're not getting the chance to play Stanley?

14. Has being in rehearsal for such a long period of time been frustrating?

15. What would make this process/production successful in your eyes?

Brooklyn Boy
Donald Margulies

ERIC

My father sold shoes. In a Buster Brown store on Sheepshead
Bay Road.

He wasn't a partner, he was an employee. For thirty-nine
years. He gave his life to that store. It wasn't even his to profit
from, yet he still gave everything to that goddamn store. I could
never understand what was so attractive about that place, why
he chose to spend so much of his days there and not at home.

I remember watching him closely in the morning, trying
to uncover the mystery of manhood, the rituals of work. The
shpritz of Aramis, the buff of the Oxfords, the tying of the perfect
Windsor knot.

I'd watch him from my window get swallowed up in the sea
of Brooklyn fathers all beginning their day.

Analysis: *Brooklyn Boy*

Type: Dramatic
Synopsis

Eric Weiss is a novelist in his midforties. Jewish, born and raised in
the Sheepshead Bay area of Brooklyn, Eric has spent a lifetime either
dodging or running away from his roots. Donald Margulies' play is
about accepting all of the aspects of our life that combine to make
us who we are, even the uncomfortable ones. We can't pick and
choose what made us, but we can accept and learn from them.

Brooklyn Boy is the title of Eric's third novel, and his most commercially successful one. Walking a fine line between fiction and memoir, it is a thinly veiled account of Eric's childhood growing up in Brooklyn and the people around him. Eric's first two novels, *The Gentleman Farmer* and *The Aerie*, were critical successes but perhaps a bit too esoteric for mass consumption. Eric's friends and relatives complain that they didn't understand what those two books were about. *Brooklyn Boy*, however, is about to reach number 11 on the *New York Times* best-seller list and Eric is launching on a national book tour.

Eric's professional life is taking off while his personal life is falling apart. He is in love with his wife, but they are getting a divorce. His father, Manny, lies dying in a Brooklyn hospital. Manny seems to be either constantly criticizing his son or not taking a vested interest in him or his work. The novel forces Eric to come to terms with his entire life.

While in Los Angeles to work out the details of the screenplay for *Brooklyn Boy*, which sold for millions of dollars, Eric picks up a young woman, Alison, at a book reading. He's living a life he's never dreamed of: rich, successful, suddenly attractive to younger women, and housed at the fancy Mondrian Hotel. Alison represents the kind of girl he never had access to in the past.

Eric finally comes to terms with everything when Manny, after dying, appears to him telling him he loves the book and that Eric got everything right. Eric realizes that who he was and who he is aren't all that different.

Character Description
Eric Weiss, 40s

Eric is a midcareer novelist in the middle of a book tour. At the beginning of the play he's made a stop in New York from Miami and on his way to L.A. The book tour consists of him travelling from store to store, reading a selection from the novel and then signing books. Eric considers this novel "serious . . . a book that aspired to be literature." It's 384 pages long and dedicated to his mother and father. It took six years to write.

Eric has spent his entire life trying to escape Brooklyn, yet his biggest success is because of his hometown. He thinks of himself like Houdini for escaping it. People from his past call him "Ricky," but those people are slowly disappearing. He and Nina, his wife, have been together since grad school, but a series of miscarriages coupled with Eric's critical, and now commercial, success have led to the demise of their marriage.

Given Circumstances
Who are they? Alison is a twenty-year-old college student who came to Eric's book signing.
Where are they? The Mondrian Hotel in Los Angeles.
When does this take place? The present.
Why are they there? Eric has brought her back to his room.
What is the pre-beat? Alison asks Eric why he wanted fame.

Questions
1. Can you state your objective in a simple, specific, and active way?
2. Who are you talking to? Be specific and have a clear image.
3. Can you think of three adjectives to describe your character?
4. Did you approach Allison, or vice versa?
5. What do you find most attractive about her?
6. Does she make you feel young, or old?
7. What does it feel like to be a critical and commercial success after all these years?

8. What's your favorite part of a book tour?

9. Have you brought women back to your room before?

10. Do you miss your wife?

11. Are you thinking about her now?

12. What does your father look like?

13. What does Aramis smell like?

14. Can you tie a Windsor knot?

15. What does "family" mean to you?

Dinner with Friends
Donald Margulies

TOM

What are you thinking? Come on, I know *you*, I know that *look* . . .

Gabe . . .

I'm trying to tell you . . . I was dying! You don't understand that, do you? I was losing the will to live, isn't that dying? The life I was leading had no relationship to who I was or what I wanted. It was deadening. The constant logistics of: "You pick up Sam and take him to lollypop tennis, I'll take Laurie to hockey practice . . . "

This is what we'd talk about! No, really. This would pass for conversation in our house.

The dog finished me off. Oh, man, that dog. Sarge. It wasn't enough that we had two cats and a guinea pig, no, Beth felt the kids had to have a dog because *she* had a dog. I'd spent my entire adult life cleaning up one form of shit or another, now I was on to *dog* shit. I should've gone into waste management. How do you keep love alive when you're shoveling shit all day long?

Analysis: *Dinner with Friends*

Type: Dramatic
Synopsis

"You never know what couples are like when they're alone; you never do."

Karen and Gabe are married. Beth and Tom are married. They live in an upscale Connecticut town. Collectively they have been a group of friends for over twelve years. In the opening scene, Beth is having dinner at Karen and Gabe's house. They've just returned from a tour of Italy. Tom is conspicuously absent. The kids play and watch a movie in another room. After a tense period, Beth finally breaks and reveals that Tom has left her and the kids for another woman. The women look at Gabe accusingly, but he had no idea about the affair. All three feel betrayed by Tom. They've grown up together, vacationed together, been pregnant together, and are raising their children together.

In scene two, we're in Beth and Tom's bedroom. Tom unexpectedly comes home because his flight was cancelled due to weather conditions. He asks Beth about dinner and then realizes she told Karen and Gabe about the divorce. He's furious. They promised to tell them together so that their friends would hear both sides of the story and not choose sides. They have a huge fight, insulting each other to the core. Beth hits Tom. He holds her down. She spits in his face. They have sex.

We're back to Karen and Gabe's house, and they're attempting to dissect the break in Beth and Tom's marriage. Karen has already taken Beth's side. Gabe is trying to remain open-minded. They're in mid-discussion when Tom shows up. This is directly after his fight (and sex) with Beth. Tom wants to explain the situation from his side. Karen doesn't want to hear it and goes to bed.

The first scene of act two flashes back to twelve years earlier. We see Karen and Gabe in the blush of being newly wedded. They're on Martha's Vineyard and they're about to play matchmaker with Beth and Tom. Beth and Tom have a rocky start. There is definitely sexual tension between the two of them, but also many, many warning signs.

The rest of the play deals with the fallout of the divorce. Karen and Beth begin to grow apart. Gabe and Tom grow apart. Karen and Gabe are forced to question the strength of their relationship, but it seems as if they'll make it.

Character Description
Tom, 40s
Tom has been married to Beth for over twelve years. They have two children together. He's been seeing (and has fallen in love with) Nancy, a travel agent. He wants a divorce so that he can be with Nancy. He tells Beth that she's "castrating," that she killed his self-confidence and refused to hear him. He feels always supported Beth on her wayward journey: getting her a nanny for the kids and building her an art studio over the garage. He did this despite the fact that he believes her art sucks and she used it as an excuse not to get a real job. Most importantly, Beth stopped touching him. He did an experiment on this. Beth went an entire week without making skin-to-skin contact.

Given Circumstances
Who are they? Gabe used to be Tom's best friend.
Where are they? A Manhattan bar.
When does this take place? The present, early evening.

Why are they there? They haven't seen each other in five months.
What is the pre-beat? Gabe has just asked Tom to explain the rules of how their conversation can proceed so he doesn't step out of bounds.

Questions

1. Can you state your objective in a simple, specific, and active way?
2. Who are you talking to? Be specific and have a clear image.
3. Can you think of three adjectives to describe your character?
4. How long have you and Gabe been friends?
5. What does he mean to you?
6. Have you tried to get together with him sooner than this?
7. Do you miss him?
8. Are you happier now without Beth?
9. How did leaving her change you?
10. How is your new life different?
11. How often do you see your kids?
12. What does Beth look like?
13. What does Nancy look like?
14. How are they different?
15. Do you think Gabe is happy? Why? Why not?

Dinner with Friends
Donald Margulies

GABE

You don't get it: I *cling* to Karen; I *cling* to her. Imagining a life without her doesn't excite me, it just makes me anxious.

It all goes by so fast, Tom, I know. The hair goes, and the waist. And the stamina; the capacity for staying up late, to read or watch a movie, never mind sex. Want to hear a shocker? Karen is premenopausal. That's right: my sweetheart, my lover, that sweet girl I lolled around with on endless Sundays, is getting hot flashes. It doesn't seem possible.

We spend our youth unconscious, feeling immortal, then we marry and have kids and awaken with a shock to mortality, theirs, ours, that's all we see. We worry about them, *their* safety, our *own*, air bags, plane crashes, pederasts, and spend our middle years wanting back the dreamy, carefree part, the part we fucked and pissed away; now we want that back, 'cause we know how fleeting it all is, now we know, and it just doesn't seem fair that so much is gone when there's really so little left. So, some of us try to regain unconsciousness. Some of us blow up our homes . . . And others of us . . . take up piano; I'm taking piano.

Analysis: *Dinner with Friends*

Type: Dramatic
Synopsis

"You never know what couples are like when they're alone; you never do."

Karen and Gabe are married. Beth and Tom are married. They live in an upscale Connecticut town. Collectively they have been a group of friends for over twelve years. In the opening scene, Beth is having dinner at Karen and Gabe's house. They've just returned from a tour of Italy. Tom is conspicuously absent. The kids play and watch a movie in another room. After a tense period Beth finally breaks and reveals that Tom has left her and the kids for another woman. The women look at Gabe accusingly, but he had no idea about the affair. All three feel betrayed by Tom. They've grown up together, vacationed together, been pregnant together, and are raising their children together.

In scene two, we're in Beth and Tom's bedroom. Tom unexpectedly comes home because his flight was cancelled due to weather conditions. He asks Beth about dinner and then realizes she told Karen and Gabe about the divorce. He's furious. They promised to tell them together so that their friends would hear both sides of the story and not choose sides. They have a huge fight, insulting each other to the core. Beth hits Tom. He holds her down. She spits in his face. They have sex.

We're back to Karen and Gabe's house, and they're attempting to dissect the break in Beth and Tom's marriage. Karen has already taken Beth's side. Gabe is trying to remain open-minded. They're in mid-discussion when Tom shows up. This is directly after his fight (and sex) with Beth. Tom wants to explain the situation from his side. Karen doesn't want to hear it and goes to bed.

The first scene of act two flashes back to twelve years earlier. We see Karen and Gabe in the blush of being newly wedded. They're on Martha's Vineyard and they're about to play matchmaker with Beth and Tom. Beth and Tom have a rocky start. There is definitely sexual tension between the two of them but also many, many warning signs.

The rest of the play deals with the fallout of the divorce. Karen and Beth begin to grow apart. Gabe and Tom grow apart. Karen and Gabe are forced to question the strength of their relationship, but it seems as if they'll make it.

Character Description
Gabe, 40s
Gabe is a foodie, obsessed with great food. Their trip to Italy was all about eating. He writes about travel and food for an unspecified publication. He is a family man. He does everything in service of his family. When Karen is driving crazily through Rome, he thinks about the future of his children without their parents. The basis of his relationship with Karen is that she talks, he writes, she edits.

Tom is his oldest friend. They met at their college freshman orientation. They have always told each other everything. Gabe is trying really hard to figure out Tom's motivations in leaving Beth, even though Gabe told Tom once he never should have married her.

Given Circumstances
Who are they? Tom used to be Gabe's best friend.
Where are they? A Manhattan bar.
When does this take place? The present, early evening.
Why are they there? They haven't seen each other in five months.
What is the pre-beat? Tom has asked Gabe if he ever wants to "chuck it all and start all over again."

Questions

1. Can you state your objective in a simple, specific, and active way?
2. Who are you talking to? Be specific and have a clear image.
3. Can you think of three adjectives to describe your character?
4. Have you been avoiding Tom for five months?
5. What does/did his friendship mean to you?
6. Can things be fixed between you, or is the break unalterable?
7. Did you think Tom and Beth belonged together forever?
8. Has this divorce made you question your marriage?
9. How long have you and Karen been together?
10. What's the first thing that comes to mind when you think about her?
11. Are you still in love with Karen?
12. Have you ever cheated?
13. Have you ever thought about cheating?
14. Do you think Tom made a mistake?
15. What are you doing here with him? What do you want?

Bad Habits
Terrence McNally

HUGH

The main thing I can tell you about Ruth Benson is that she was fat. About 280, I'd say.

I mean, she was circus fat.

What else about her? I think Ruth Benson is the only person, man, woman or child, I ever asked to take a bath. She used to smoke six packs a day, minimum. Cigarillos. Nicotine stains right up to her elbow! I don't guess she ever drew a sober breath.

My main image of her is passed out on the floor like a big rancid mountain. And talk about being a slob! She had dustballs under her bed the size of watermelons. She didn't have roaches in her kitchen. She raised them. It was like a goddamn stud farm in there. You'd light the oven and there'd be a flash-fire from all the grease.

She was an out and out pig.

We had a lot in common, Ruthie and I. I'll never forget the night we each caught the other precisely the same instant picking their nose. God, she was gross. Just thinking of her with all those fingers up there and I have to smile. You're bringing back a lot of bad memories, Nurse. I haven't thought of Ruth Benson and her soiled sheets in a long time.

Analysis: *Bad Habits*

Type: Comedic
Synopsis

Bad Habits is a wicked black comedy dealing with addiction, mental health, and the health-care industry.

In act one Dolly comes to Ravenswood, a rehabilitation retreat for couples seeking therapy and relationship counseling, on a sudden urge to visit her husband Harry. Harry has put himself under the care of Dr. Jason Pepper. Dolly has been reading Pepper's book on the subject, *Marriage for the Fun of It!* While most couples come to Ravenswood together, Harry came on his own and has been here for months.

Dr. Pepper has been wheelchair-bound ever since his ex-wife threw him down a staircase. He runs the retreat with a fairly lax and mostly unorthodox hand. He encourages his patients to drink heavily, smoke heavily, and maintain high-calorie diets. Some of the patients here have been under his care for years. He treats all couples: male/female, male/male, female/female.

The outcome of his months of therapy is that Harry doesn't want to kill Dolly anymore.

Act two centers on Dunelawn, a facility for people battling addictions: drinking, smoking, dressing in drag. It is run by the always silent Dr. Toynbee. He has two female nurses on staff who do all of the work; their names are Benson and Hedges. Hedges makes the observation that none of the patients here ever seem to get better. When the patients get the urge to act on their addiction, the nurses inject them with a serum that temporarily soothes the desire.

Character Description
Hugh Gumbs, 40s

Hugh smokes five packs of cigarettes a day. Some nights he sets his alarm to wake him at fifteen-minute intervals for smokes. He says that he's here solely for his nicotine addiction, but he is also a compulsive liar, a kleptomaniac, a womanizer, and a drinker. He whispers his worst addiction in Dr. Toynbee's ear. The doctor is so appalled that he leaves without looking at Hugh. He is recently divorced.

In this monologue he's describing Ruth Benson to Ruth Benson, unaware that it's her. After this encounter she admits that she changed completely for him. She asks him if could ever love her. Hugh replies that if he didn't love her when she was fat and rotten, he can't love her now that she's beautiful and perfect and has such terrific legs.

Given Circumstances

Who are they? Hugh is talking to an unrecognizable Ruth Benson.
Where are they? The grounds of Dunelawn, an addiction recovery center.
When does this take place? The present.
Why are they there? Hugh is in recovery; Ruth is a nurse there.
What is the pre-beat? Ruth says he was raving about "Ruth Benson" the other night and she must be very important to him.

Questions

1. Can you state your objective in a simple, specific, and active way?
2. Who are you talking to? Be specific and have a clear image.
3. Can you think of three adjectives to describe your character?
4. Has Nurse Benson taken good care of you?
5. What is your worst addiction?

6. How does smoking make you feel?
7. Do you really want to quit?
8. How long have you been at Dunelawn?
9. Is it helping?
10. Do you recognize your habits as destructive?
11. What does Dr. Toynbee look like?
12. Do you like him?
13. Do you miss your wife?
14. How long were you married?
15. Why did you divorce?

Elemeno Pea
Molly Smith Metzler

ETHAN

What, you mean Simone? We weren't set up. I mean, I think
Peter had mentioned Simone in a vague way—he said she
went to Yale like we all did, blahdy blah—but I didn't pay it
any mind until I met her on Xmas Eve.

No, Simone wasn't *working*, she was a guest. She came
down their marble staircase in a red strapless Vera gown and
knocked me right outta my chair. It was quite an entrance,
believe you me.

I teased her that she *must've* choreographed the whole
thing—with the *descent* into the room, some strategically-
placed tinsel caught in her hair. But now that I know her, I
know she was just Simone being Simone. She has no idea how
people stare at her and want to be next to her. It's because she's
so *good*. She's good and sweet and let me tell you something
I've learned about myself, Dora . . . Derot . . . FUCK! Why
can't I get this?! Is it an unusual name?

Devon. Devon, Kevin, Devon, Kevin. Let me tell you something I've learned about myself, *Kevin*: I *want* good and sweet
and innocent and kind. Women spend hundreds of thousands
of dollars on plastic surgery trying to get what Simone has—but
you can't buy what she's got. Because it like comes through
her skin or something. I mean, look at her.

I was on my Berry when Simone came down those stairs
and you know what, Devon? I didn't even say goodbye to

whoever I was talking to or anything. Just: There's Simone.
End call.

Analysis: *Elemeno Pea*

Type: Seriocomic
Synopsis
The action takes place on a beach estate, on a bluff, in Martha's
Vineyard, just after Labor Day. There is a main house, a guest house,
and servants' quarters. Michaela and Peter Kell are the owners of the
estate, and Simone is Michaela's personal assistant. Michaela is
letting Simone have a girls' weekend with her sister, Devon. Simone
and Devon are staying in the guest house. It is equipped with voice-
activated iTunes in the ceiling, and floor-to-ceiling glass walls that
lead onto a wraparound porch with an amazing view. These people
have a lot of money.

Simone and Devon are from Buffalo, New York. They are total
opposites. Simone is beautiful, tan, and poised. She makes a lot of
money working for Michaela and she is also writing a novel. Devon
is at a low point in her life. Recently divorced, working a terrible
low-paying job, and sleeping in her parents' basement, she is overwhelmed by the wealth here. Devon spends the play constantly
reminding Simone that she is the "help" and that she's deserted her
family on numerous occasions for strangers.

This is a world unlike any Simone and Devon have known. Devon
doesn't understand Michaela or her sense of entitlement. She also
doesn't understand how Simone has let Michaela bribe her with
money, gifts, and trips in order to stay. Michaela is going through
some really difficult marital trouble. She offers Devon a substantial
amount of money ($10,000) to leave. Devon refuses, although she
takes the check.

From that moment on, Devon uses every opportunity to undermine Michaela. She invites the groundskeeper, called Jos-B because there is another man named José who works on the property, to dinner. When Ethan walks in, Devon sizes him up immediately and realizes she knows nothing about her sister, who has seemed to abandon all her dreams on account of money.

When Michaela reveals to Devon the tragedy of her husband forcing her to get an abortion because tests showed something wrong with the baby, Devon finally sees her and the two find common ground. Simone, on the other hand, decides to go off on a boat trip with Ethan, leaving all the problems behind her.

Character Description
Ethan, early 40s
Ethan is Peter's best friend but puts on the facade of being Michaela's friend, as well. He's handsome, sun-kissed, and upper class. He has $200 blond highlights in his hair. When he arrives at the house he brings three bouquets of roses, one for each woman. When Michaela grills him about Peter's whereabouts, he initially lies. He finally comes clean and tells her he was at the "club" with him and that Peter is going to leave her. He loves to travel internationally, "immersing himself in other cultures." He has a seventy-five-foot sailboat named *Ethan II*. He went to Yale but doesn't have a job—he doesn't need one.

Given Circumstances
Who are they? Devon is Simone's sister.
Where are they? A beach estate on Martha's Vineyard.
When does this take place? The present.
Why are they there? Ethan has come to break the news to Michaela that her marriage is over.

What is the pre-beat? Devon makes a comment about Ethan having been "set up" with Simone.

Questions

1. Can you state your objective in a simple, specific, and active way?
2. Who are you talking to? Be specific and have a clear image.
3. Can you think of three adjectives to describe your character?
4. How long have you and Simone been together?
5. Do you love her?
6. What is her most attractive feature?
7. Is the age difference between the two of you a plus, or a problem?
8. Does Devon look anything like Simone?
9. Do they have any similar personality traits?
10. Do you enjoy not having to work?
11. How do you fill your days?
12. Are you going to marry Simone?
13. Does Peter and Michaela's failing marriage give you pause?
14. Do you like Michaela?
15. What's the urgency behind this monologue?

We All Knew It Was Coming
Allison Moore

ALEX

We all knew it was coming. But the best minds, the smartest people on the planet were on the job. They were gonna fix it, that's what they kept saying. They were gonna literally save the world.

In other places the crazy cults appeared, especially after the first intercept failed. I saw it on the news, the mass suicides, looting, riots. But somehow, we avoided most of that. I mean, it turns out Garrison Keillor was right. Minnesotans don't really go in for that sorta thing.

In our neighborhood, it was really quiet. Northeast is an old Polish neighborhood, very working class. Small houses with long, narrow lots. Most people didn't have fences, so you could see your neighbors in their yards. And as it got closer, we all drifted outside to watch.

And I'm holding my son in my arms. He keeps putting his hands on my face, pressing his little palms against my cheeks as we look at the sky. And when the meteor appears, streaking toward its target it is so . . . silent. There are no cars, no sounds of traffic. Just the hum of the power lines and our collective breathing, each in our own patch of grass as we watch this slow motion collision happening millions of miles away.

And when it strikes the moon, I feel it, in my veins, my organs, all the water in me being pulled with it, the way my son pulls on my arm, until his hand slips, and the invisible line

snaps, and the moon disappears from sight, released from orbit,
careening off into the ever-expanding universe.

And we are left standing in our yards in the dark.

Analysis: *We All Knew It Was Coming*

Type: Dramatic
Synopsis and Character Description

This piece was written as a stand-alone monologue, so all of the
factual information you need about the character and events can be
found within. It was part of a collection of pieces commissioned by
the Humana Festival dealing with the end of the world.

Alex is a dad in his forties. He lives in the Midwest, specifically
in Minnesota. The age of Alex's son is unknown, as is the status/loca-
tion of his wife.

Alex says, "we all knew it was coming" and later references a meteor making its way toward the moon. So it appears that the world is
prepared for this monumental event. In fact, scientists attempted to
intercept the meteor but failed. There's nothing to do now but watch
and wait.

In other parts of the world people are rioting, looting, killing
themselves, taking advantage of the end or taking control of their
fate.

Alex starts with a global perspective and then brings it closer to
home, talking about his neighborhood and, finally, about his son.

The fact that Alex is recounting this event in retrospect means
that he survived the disaster, but at what cost, and what world is he
left living in? The event manages to be communal and individual at
the same time. It's life-changing.

In order to truly craft this monologue you need to 100 percent
believe you've experienced an event that potentially meant the end

of the world. Look most specifically at the language Alex uses to describe his body at the moment the meteor made contact with moon. It's very vivid and visceral.

Given Circumstances

Who are they? Alex is talking to the audience.

Where are they? Minnesota.

When does this take place? Mid- or post-apocalypse.

Why are they there? He is watching the sky.

What is the pre-beat? This is a stand-alone monologue.

Questions

1. Can you state your objective in a simple, specific, and active way?
2. Who are you talking to? Be specific and have a clear image.
3. Can you think of three adjectives to describe your character?
4. "The audience" isn't specific enough. Who could you be speaking to?
5. Where in Minnesota are you, and how big is your town?
6. How old is your child? Is he safe?
7. Where is your wife?
8. Is your home still standing?
9. What did the apocalypse sound like?
10. What did it feel like?
11. Are you scared?
12. Was there advance warning of the event?
13. What is your plan for the future?
14. What was your career pre-apocalypse?
15. Are you happy you survived?

Butterfly Kiss
Phyllis Nagy

TEDDY

I'm doing push-ups on Jones Beach and believe me, I'm trying to forget the cold. Up walks Sloan Ross and his baby. I say to the baby, how do you do? I'm Teddy Roosevelt Hayes and I'm an ex-Marine. She says, hi there, Teddy. I'm Lily Ross. Do you think I'm fat?

I'm staring at this little girl with slim hips . . . but real slim . . . and all I can picture is how she's gonna have one hell of a time in childbirth with hips like those.

I say to her, well, Lily, seems to me you've got the slimmest hips this side of heaven and she grins, leans in real close so I can see her tits and says, well, Teddy, what do you think about THAT?

Sloanie's having a grand time embarrassing me in front of his kid. I spend the day covering myself up with a beach towel. Sloanie keeps asking, hey, Teddy, what's the deal with the *towel*? Like he knows I'm hiding something. And I am. Middle of November and this girl child with slim hips is running around Jones Beach in a bathing suit.

She's collecting seashells and wriggling her tight little ass in my face. What was I supposed to do? I'm a pretty normal guy. Never been arrested. Never taken much more than a social drink. And I'd certainly never been moved to excitement by fourteen-year-old buns. But Lily Ross . . . well. She was . . . exciting to me.

I tried to put it out of mind. Sloanie knew what was going on. He probably planned it. Slim hips. My my my . . . Lily Ross was a sweetheart. Can't believe she went and popped her mommy off that way.

Analysis: *Butterfly Kiss*

Type: Dramatic
Synopsis

The action of the play focuses on Lily Ross, a twenty-something resident of New York City. Lily works at a small gift shop at the South Street Seaport, but her real interest is musical composition. Lily grew up on a matriarchal household surrounded by her mother and grand-mother. At the opening of the play, Lily is in prison for allegedly killing her mother.

The story bounces back and forth between the present and the past as Nagy slowly reveals the depths of Lily's psyche and the hold she has over the people in her life. Lily is an enigma, and everyone wants her and wants to know more about her.

Lily spends her time in prison reading up on famous, sensational murder cases. She then relays the stories to Martha, her lover, when she visits. Lily tells Martha she wants to write an opera.

Sloan, Lily's father, is a lepidopterist, mostly absent, and has a lover. Jenny, Lily's mother, stays home all day. Sloan may have arranged for the barely teenaged Lily to seduce his best friend Teddy because he likes to scientifically observe things.

Jenny treats Lily more like a sister than a daughter. Jenny's generalized anxieties increase once she suspects Sloan of having an affair. Jenny slowly starts to lose her mind. She asks the same questions over and over. She believes Lily lives with a man. She thinks Lily is pregnant and wants her to name the baby Jenny, after her. She wants Lily to write songs for her.

One day, while Lily is brushing Jenny's hair, she takes Sloan's gun out of the bedside table and coaxes Jenny into asking for death. This scene is the final one in the play, and Nagy leaves it to the audience to decide whether Jenny wants to die or not.

Character Description
Teddy, mid- to late 40s
His full name is Theodore Roosevelt Hays. Teddy was Lily's first lover. He's a former Marine, big and handsome but a little slow on the uptake. He's sweeter and more polite than one would expect. Lily calls him "the dumbest man" she knows but sweet and uncomplicated. He met Sloan, Lily's father, when they served in the Marines together. They reunite every year.

When Teddy meets Lily he has a fourteen-year-old girl of his own named Eleanor. This doesn't stop him from having the affair with Lily.

He doesn't know for certain if he's named after President Theodore Roosevelt. He never asked and it never came up.

Given Circumstances
Who are they? Teddy is talking to the police.

Where are they? It's not specified in the text.

When does this take place? The present.

Why are they there? The police are investigating the death of Lily's mother.

What is the pre-beat? This is a stand-alone monologue.

Questions

1. Can you state your objective in a simple, specific, and active way?
2. Who are you talking to? Be specific and have a clear image.
3. Can you think of three adjectives to describe your character?
4. How long did your affair with Lily last?
5. Were you concerned about Lily's age when the affair began?
6. Do you think Sloan arranged the meeting between you and Lily on purpose?
7. Are you and Sloan still friends?
8. When is the last time you spoke with or saw Lily?
9. Do you believe she could have killed her mother?
10. Is physical fitness still important to you?
11. What business are you in?
12. Does this monologue happen at your business, your home, or the police station?
13. Are you still married?
14. Do you love your wife?
15. Are you still attracted to Lily?

What Didn't Happen
Christopher Shinn

PETER

Speaking of pathology . . . I'd like to lay David on the couch for a moment. May I, David?

Thank you. We're in the market just now, buying some meat, and I remark, "That's a very nice shirt, David." "Yes," he says, "isn't it? But I bought it from Banana Republic, and I can't shop there anymore because they use sweatshop labor."

It's the same thing at cocktail parties, when I hear people speaking in serious hushed tones about Bosnia. "I can't believe we're not doing anything more," they say. "We should be doing something." We, *we*? It's "they" who do things—governments, corporations, "we" have no "power," no effect on history that way, what's all this "we" talk?

But we just elected a President who went on *60 Minutes* with his wife in a headband and told us he was a bad man in his "personal behavior," and we voted for him anyway. I think that's progress! (Lucky she wore that ugly castrating thing, else people might not have sympathized.) But really, it's a new age, and you just have to resign yourself to it, David: we're small creatures in a vast, unfathomable world, a world that spins forward despite us, and whether or not one buys a shirt at Banana Republic is a superfluous dilemma. The shirt is made! What we don't have control over: *that* is history. What we *do* have control over: that is *pleasure*.

Analysis: *What Didn't Happen*

Type: Seriocomic
Synopsis

The action of the play takes place around a house in upstate New York in 1999 and 1993. Scott and Jamie, his daughter, have recently moved into the house. The purchase of the home was impulsive. Scott's ex-wife is in Europe. He has taken his daughter to three therapists to find out what is wrong with her. He's depressed in his career as a television producer. He needed a change. Emily, his head writer, comes up for the weekend to work on a script with Scott. They have an intimate relationship the boundaries of which remain undefined.

In flashbacks to 1993 we see Scott, an aspiring writer, as the caretaker of this property, owned by Dave, a novelist, who bought the house in 1983. The grounds used to be used to shear and slaughter sheep. Peter, also a novelist and riding the waves of his newfound success, drives up for the day for dinner. Peter brings with him Elaine, an actress, who is Dave's current girlfriend. Peter and Dave are friends, but they haven't seen each other in a while, perhaps because of Peter's success. More people show up for dinner, upsetting Elaine, who hasn't seen Dave in three months and expected time alone together. She needs to talk to him about their relationship.

The evening explodes when Peter suggests to Dave that he start writing about his own life, his own struggles, because he is smarter and more interesting than his books. Peter also lets slip that Dave's publishers are opting out of their contract because Dave is so much trouble. Then Scott and Elaine kiss and Dave kicks Scott out.

Flash-forward to 1999 and Scott has turned himself into a seemingly more successful version of Dave. He also has a young caretaker very much like himself whom he's mentoring.

Character Description
Peter Lawson, 40s
Peter is a successful novelist. His two books are titled *Tall Grass* and *Laura on the Jitney*. In 1993 he's known Dave for ten years, but hasn't seen him in a year. He didn't know that Dave bought this house. He didn't want to come empty-handed so he picked up a bottle of wine. He also has a country house in a slightly more upscale section of New York where everyone "wears the same shoes." Peter refers to himself as a boob. He's married to Mary and they have a thirteen-year-old son. His friends describe him as "up" and "fun." Recently, one of his books was turned into a film and it opened his work up to a whole new audience. He drives a Volvo and drinks scotch. Peter has spent his entire life trying to be an intellectual but he's not, he's a charming smartass. He finds writing, sitting in a room for twelve hours a day, lonely and unbearable.

Given Circumstances
Who are they? Old friends who haven't seen each other in a while.
Where are they? On the grounds of Dave's upstate New York home.
When does this take place? 1993.
Why are they there? Peter was driving upstate so offered Elaine a ride.
What is the pre-beat? Alan, a professor and stranger to Peter, makes a statement about the difference between theory and art.

Questions
1. Can you state your objective in a simple, specific, and active way?
2. Who are you talking to? Be specific and have a clear image.
3. Can you think of three adjectives to describe your character?
4. What's kept you from seeing Dave for the past ten years?
5. Do you miss him?

6. Are you supportive friends? Competitive?
7. Can you describe your writing?
8. Do you write every day?
9. Do you drink while you write?
10. Do you think Dave could be more successful?
11. Is he a better writer than you?
12. Has success changed you at all?
13. Why are you a boob?
14. How long have you been married?
15. Are you still in love with Mary?

What Didn't Happen
Christopher Shinn

PETER

When they were arranging my book tour, I told them I wanted
to branch out—develop a bigger audience, so I told them not to
send me to Boston and L.A. and Chicago. The real reason was
that I was ashamed of the book. I went to cities like Pittsburgh
and Ann Arbor, where I knew no one. I was also really fat.

Well. I am in Minneapolis. I give my reading. Afterwards,
a middle-aged woman—a bit softer than middle-aged actually,
but no longer young—this woman—who is black—approaches
me. With a big bright nervous face. And tells me how much
my books mean to her.

I'm aghast, as I've never before been approached by a black
reader. I ask her why she likes my books and she laughs as though
it's a preposterous question. "Because they're good. They make
me cry," she says. I want to know more, so I say, "But why?" I'm
thinking, What does this woman relate to in my work? My books
are about rich white people. She says, "Same shit goes on
where I work, people hurting each other, stabbing each other
in the back, this one slept with that one, this one's treating that
one wrong, and everyone's doing their best but it just falls apart,
and it's left like that, no way to put it back together."

So I invite her to walk with me to my hotel. She does. I say,
"Come to my room and have a cup of tea." She comes in. I
make tea. We sit at the cheap shiny coffee table. I say, "I'd like
to kiss you."

And quite calmly, quite sweetly, not an ounce of condescension in her voice: she says, "I think you'll be just fine in a few minutes for not having done that." And she smiles an extraordinary smile. As do I. And she is gone.

Because. Do you? . . . For so many years I felt. Doubt and. *Guilt.* Over my work—over my life. And to see—as I sat there with her—ghost—in the room. I thought of her wisdom.

Which so eclipsed mine.

Analysis: *What Didn't Happen*

Type: Dramatic
Synopsis

The action of the play takes place around a house in upstate New York in 1999 and 1993. Scott and Jamie, his daughter, have recently moved into the house. The purchase of the home was impulsive. Scott's ex-wife is in Europe. He has taken his daughter to three therapists to find out what is wrong with her. He's depressed in his career as a television producer. He needed a change. Emily, his head writer, comes up for the weekend to work on a script with Scott. They have an intimate relationship the boundaries of which remain undefined.

In flashbacks to 1993 we see Scott, an aspiring writer, as the caretaker of this property, owned by Dave, a novelist, who bought the house in 1983. The grounds used to be used to shear and slaughter sheep. Peter, also a novelist and riding the waves of his newfound success, drives up for the day for dinner. Peter brings with him Elaine, an actress, who is Dave's current girlfriend. Peter and Dave are friends, but they haven't seen each other in a while, perhaps because of Peter's success. More people show up for dinner, upsetting Elaine, who hasn't seen Dave in three months and expected time alone together. She needs to talk to him about their relationship.

The evening explodes when Peter suggests to Dave that he start writing about his own life, his own struggles, because he is smarter and more interesting than his books. Peter also lets slip that Dave's publishers are opting out of their contract because Dave is so much trouble. Then Scott and Elaine kiss and Dave kicks Scott out.

Flash-forward to 1999 and Scott has turned himself into a seemingly more successful version of Dave. He also has a young caretaker very much like himself whom he's mentoring.

Character Description
Peter Lawson, 40s

Peter is a successful novelist. His two books are titled *Tall Grass* and *Laura on the Jitney*. In 1993 he's known Dave for ten years, but hasn't seen him in a year. He didn't know that Dave bought this house. He didn't want to come empty-handed so he picked up a bottle of wine. He also has a country house in a slightly more upscale section of New York where everyone "wears the same shoes." Peter refers to himself as a boob. He's married to Mary and they have a thirteen-year-old son. His friends describe him as "up" and "fun." Recently, one of his books was turned into a film and it opened his work up to a whole new audience. He drives a Volvo and drinks scotch. Peter has spent his entire life trying to be an intellectual but he's not, he's a charming smartass. He finds writing, sitting in a room for twelve hours a day, lonely and unbearable.

Given Circumstances

Who are they? Peter is talking to Dave and Scott, Dave's protégé.
Where are they? The grounds of Dave's upstate New York house.
When does this take place? 1993.
Why are they there? Peter was driving upstate so offered Elaine a ride.

What is the pre-beat? Peter has just let slip that Dave's publishers are optioning out of their contract with Dave.

Questions

1. Can you state your objective in a simple, specific, and active way?
2. Who are you talking to? Be specific and have a clear image.
3. Can you think of three adjectives to describe your character?
4. Was the slip about Dave's option accidental, or intentional?
5. What has kept you and Dave apart for a year?
6. Are you enjoying your success?
7. Do you think it's deserved?
8. Is Dave a better writer than you?
9. What's the best part of touring?
10. Have you picked up women on tour before?
11. Do you cheat on your wife?
12. Are you still in love with her?
13. How long have the two of you been together?
14. Do you have an idea for your next book?
15. How did the experience you related in this monologue change you?

The Curious Incident of the Dog in the Night-Time
Simon Stephens

ED

How are you feeling? Can I get you anything?

Look maybe I shouldn't say this, but . . . I want you to know that you can trust me . . . You have to know that I am going to tell you the truth from now on. About everything. Because . . . if you don't tell the truth now, then later on it hurts even more.

So . . . I killed Wellington, Christopher. Just . . . let me explain.

When your mum left . . . Eileen . . . Mrs. Shears . . . she was very good to me. She helped me through a very difficult time. Well, you know how she was round here most days. I thought . . . Well . . . Shit Christopher, I'm trying to keep this simple . . . I thought she might carry on coming over . . . I thought . . . and maybe I was being stupid . . . I thought she might . . . eventually . . . want to move in here. Or that we might move into her house. I thought we were friends. And I guess I thought wrong.

We argued Christopher, and . . . She said some things I'm not going to say to you because they're not nice . . . I think she cared more for that bloody dog than for us. And maybe that's not so stupid looking back. Maybe it's easier living on your own looking after some stupid mutt, than sharing your life with other actual human beings. I mean, shit, buddy, we're not exactly low maintenance, are we?

Anyway, we had this row. And after this particularly nasty little blow-out, she chucked me out of the house. And you know what that bloody dog was like. Nice as pie one moment, roll over, tickle its stomach. Sink its teeth into your leg the next. Anyway we're yelling at each other and it's in the garden. So when she slams the door behind me the bugger's waiting for me.

And . . . I know, I know. Maybe if I'd just given it a kick it would probably have backed off. But, shit Christopher, when the red mist comes down . . . Christ, you know what I'm talking about. I mean we're not that different me and you. And it was like everything I'd been bottling up for two years just . . .

I never meant for it to turn out like this.

Analysis: *The Curious Incident of the Dog in the Night-Time*

Type: Dramatic
Synopsis

The play opens with Christopher standing over the dead body of Wellington, a dog belonging to his neighbor, Mrs. Shears. Wellington has a large garden fork sticking out of his side.

The events of the play are being read aloud by Siobhan, Christopher's high school teacher. She serves as both narrator and character throughout the story. Christopher has an unstated medical condition that severely affects his ability to relate to people physically and emotionally. Although the condition is never stated, it bears a strong resemblance to Asperger's syndrome, or high-functioning autism.

When the police come to investigate, an officer attempts to touch Christopher, who hits him. Christopher's father, Ed, comes to the station to retrieve Christopher and explain his condition to the police.

They let him go. Christopher vows to find Wellington's murderer, even though Ed tells him to let it go. Christopher's investigation leads him down a path of discovery he never could have expected. He begins by going door-to-door in his neighborhood. Mrs. Shears won't speak to him. A kindly older woman, Mrs. Alexander, tries to befriend him.

Christopher believes his mother died two years ago. That's what his father told him. First Christopher finds out his mother was having an affair with Mr. Shears. Then he finds stacks of letters his mother has written to Christopher, some very recent, in Ed's room. She is alive and living in London with Mr. Shears.

He is detailing the events around his investigation in a notebook, which is what Siobhan is reading to us. Ed tells Christopher he threw his notebook away. While Christopher is searching for the notebook, he finds the letters and gets very upset and very sick. This is when Ed finds him. Their relationship is permanently altered.

Christopher swipes his father's debit card and leaves his small town of Swindon to find his mother in London—which he does.

Ed comes to London and finds him, forcing a sort of reunion among the family. Christopher chooses to stay with his mother but slowly begins to let Ed back into his life. Ultimately Christopher passes his A-level. Ed gets a puppy to give Christopher a reason to come over more.

Character Description
Ed, 40s
Ed is raising Christopher on his own. He wants his son to keep his nose out of other people's business. Ed lied to Christopher about his wife, Judy, dying. He finds Christopher's notebook, reads it, and is furious at the history his son has uncovered (i.e., his wife's affair). He hits Christopher in his fury and instantly regrets it. He has

developed a way to touch and calm Christopher: Ed holds up his left hand and spreads his fingers. Christopher does the same with his right. Then they touch fingers and thumbs.

Given Circumstances

Who are they? Christopher is Ed's teenaged son.

Where are they? Ed's home.

When does this take place? The present.

Why are they there? It's their home.

What is the pre-beat? Christopher has discovered forty-three letters his mother sent that Ed hid.

Questions

1. Can you state your objective in a simple, specific, and active way?
2. Who are you talking to? Be specific and have a clear image.
3. Can you think of three adjectives to describe your character?
4. What did Wellington look like?
5. Was he a good dog?
6. What did Mrs. Shears say to you exactly?
7. Do you feel guilty about killing Wellington?
8. Do you love Christopher?
9. What is it like raising him alone?
10. What is the best thing about Christopher?
11. What is the most frustrating thing about him?
12. When is the last time you saw Judy?
13. Do you miss her?
14. Do you still love her?
15. Why did you hide all her letters to Christopher?

Greedy
Kathryn Walat

AVERY

I look like Barak Obama. People have been telling me that since the 2004 Democratic National Convention, when he made that *speech*, and everyone started saying things like: "One day, that man will be . . . " But that was just something to say. Come on, you never really thought it would happen—not so soon, did you?

Things come fast: like the summer when we lose it all.

So now I look like the President of the United States, and then there's the smoking thing. We both like to say we've quit, but watch—the way his fingers do that, very subtle—near the end of a long press conference, and all I can think is: Me too, Barak. Me too.

[*He looks down at his empty fingers. Longing. Looks back up at us.*]

I don't believe in race. You look at me, and you think you see a black man, and that probably means all kinds of shit to you. But that's your shit. To me, inside my skin, race—is meaningless. Like this fine cashmere sweater . . .

[*He takes off his sweater, and deliberately drops it on the ground.*]

Just something I wear, part of the performance.

[*He removes his brown leather shoes, lovingly. He wears no socks.*]

Cole Haan. On my professor's salary, a bit ridiculous, I know. But see how nicely they match my skin color? Do you want me to keep going?

Ann Arbor is cold. This winter I practically froze my dick off. New York summers are hot. Africa's hot—sweaty, but we're not here to talk about my dick, or Barak, or my skin.

Take it in. Take me in. Please.

Analysis: *Greedy*

Type: Seriocomic
Synopsis and Character Description

This piece was written as a stand-alone monologue, so all of the factual information you need about the character and events can be found within.

Avery is a forty-something black man who looks like President Barak Obama. He is a professor, but we're not told what his field of study is. Not only does Avery look like the president, but he also has quit smoking. He can see the signs of need and addiction in the president's twitchy fingers.

Avery makes a passing remark about "the summer we lose it all." It's up to you to decide what exactly that means, but it must be pretty important; a major life event. Given the title of the piece is *Greedy*, it leads me to believe that Avery is referencing his job, his home, his family, his security, all of the things that mean a comfortable life. What precipitated this loss—and has he recovered?

At the same time, Avery references his fine cashmere sweater and his Cole Haan shoes, items that, individually, can cost hundreds of dollars. If he has lost everything, why is he spending money on brand-name clothing?

Avery says he doesn't believe in race. What does he mean by this statement, and what does he believe in? Can he look at someone who is white, Asian, Middle Eastern, et cetera, and not see the color of their skin?

He refers to the clothing that he wears as "part of the performance," almost as if they're items in a costume. Then what is the show, and who is Avery playing, and who is the audience?

It seems clear that Avery is struggling with being seen as an individual. If the monologue continued, it seems that he would take off all his clothes and stand naked before his audience. What does he want us to know about him?

Given Circumstances

Who are they? Avery is talking to the audience.

Where are they? It is not specified in the text.

When does this take place? The present.

Why are they there? You have to make a specific, high-stakes decision as it's not stated in the text.

What is the pre-beat? As this is a stand-alone piece, you need to make a decision.

Questions

1. Can you state your objective in a simple, specific, and active way?
2. Who are you talking to? Be specific and have a clear image.
3. Can you think of three adjectives to describe your character?
4. Who could you be talking to? Your class? Your boss? The police?
5. What subject do you teach?
6. Do you like your job?
7. Do you teach at a top-tier school?

8. How much money do you make a year?

9. Is your position stable?

10. Do you supplement your income in any way?

11. Are you greedy? Or are you reacting to the greed of the people around you?

12. Do you always feel like you're performing?

13. How is this particular performance different from any other day?

14. Are you married?

15. Are you in love?

Ancient Gods of the Backwoods
Kathryn Walat

KARL

There are three things you need to know about being a man around here.

[*He pauses. Thinking. Recalibrating.*]

I'd like to say these are universal truths, but I don't know. I can only speak about the particular: this barroom, this town—this *part* of town, really—this side of the tracks. And in the woods out yonder, anything goes there: the law of the wild, which is exactly what I'm talking about here.

Number one. Have restraint. Not in a gentleman-like way. Nothing gentle about what I'm talking about here. You hold back because you know it's going to be yours.

And there's something wonderful and—juicy—like sweet, sweet lemonade—about that knowledge. You've got a deer in your sight. You track it. You steady your finger on the trigger, don't want to pull too soon—you want to hold out for the best shot—the clean through—you want to watch her move a little bit, nibble some grass, wag her tail, sip her drink—watch her across the bar, knowing that by the end of the night, she will be . . .

Number two, a man's word is a man's word, and once you say something, never back down. Self-explanatory. I don't care how stupid or drunk you were when you said it. Same goes for your buddies. You stand by them in their most misguided notions.

Now, I'm speaking to you like a son here—

Right. That's what I mean. Son. My only son. And that's why this matters so much.

Analysis: *Ancient Gods of the Backwoods*

Type: Seriocomic
Synopsis

The action of the play takes place in a land that's off the beaten track. It's not pretty and it's rural—a place the god's don't give a shit about. Just because the gods have forgotten about these people doesn't mean they don't exist. The town even has an oracle, although it's covered with beer cans and graffiti.

It's hunting season, and the men went out to the woods the previous weekend—and not all of them came back. Anne's two brothers died while hunting. Her mother, who owned the bar, hanged herself. Anne's father blinded himself. Walat references Greek mythology not only in the title, but in the action of the play. This story is an attempt by Anne to take control of her entire life, on an epic scale. Her family seems to be tragically fucked. She's trying to figure out if she needs to be, as well.

Anne tries to have sex with Damon, her boyfriend, in the forest, but he says the time isn't right. She always wants to do things when she's ready. He works at Karl's bar and has to get to work, so there probably isn't enough time. Damon dreams of opening a landscaping business.

Karl is getting the bar in order. Although maintaining the business is important, it's the illegal numbers game that happens in the bar that's more important.

Anne thinks the deer that Karl shot is calling to her for a proper burial. She wants Jackie to help her bury it before Karl hangs its head in the bar. Jackie won't help her, so Anne steals the deer, cuts off its antlers, and buries it—but not very deeply. Karl is furious. She says the gods made her do it. Karl tells Damon he has to punish Anne for her betrayal.

Walat is exploring the idea of free will versus destiny: how much of our lives are really in our control.

Jackie, knowing that Karl is going to go after Anne, comes into the bar with a shotgun, and instead of being a chicken shit, she shoots and kills him. Then she turns to Anne for guidance, because Anne is the one who always knows what to do.

Character Description
Karl, 40s
Karl runs a bar and a numbers game. Damon is his eighteen-year-old, sensitive son. He is guardian to Anne, his sixteen-year-old "niece." They aren't actually blood relatives. Karl's nephews were killed while hunting the previous weekend, and Karl seemed more concerned with the deer he shot than the boys. He likes to play darts. He's very well endowed. Damon is his son. He wants to get the bar in order. The real business is the illicit business that happens in the bar, not the selling of booze. The deer he shot is going to get hung in the bar as a sign that you don't fuck with Karl. He sucker punches Damon in the stomach to prove a point. He points his gun at Anne. He's a bit of a bully.

Given Circumstances
Who are they? Karl is talking to himself, rehearsing a speech to his son.
Where are they? The bar.
When does this take place? The present, hunting season.
Why are they there? Karl now runs the bar.
What is the pre-beat? This is the beginning of the scene.

Questions

1. Can you state your objective in a simple, specific, and active way?
2. Who are you talking to? Be specific and have a clear image.
3. Can you think of three adjectives to describe your character?
4. What do you like about hunting?
5. Do you drink a lot?
6. What's your alcohol of choice?
7. How long have you been running the bar?
8. Has that always been your dream?
9. How far did you get in school?
10. What happened to your wife?
11. What does Damon look like?
12. Do you love him?
13. Who taught you to be a man?
14. Do you exercise restraint?
15. What's the urgency behind this monologue?

Brontosaurus
Lanford Wilson

ANTIQUES DEALER

I read somewhere that every ounce of alcohol you drink kills four thousand brain cells which are not regenerated. Contrary to what I read somewhere else.

I understand that rather than being a steady, every-night tippler, it's healthier, or less destructive, really, to go on a monthly all out binge. Which is worth considering if one is interested in being less destructive. Which maybe I am; despite appearances.

Nephew of mine, my house is yours.

Please make friends. Bring them here. I like young people. I like people, though I don't seem to sometimes. "People," you understand, no specific person. Bring them here. The "apartment" is yours. It's been photographed for every classy publication from *Abitare* to the *Sunday Times Magazine* and in not one picture has there been a living soul. Large, flat colorless rooms in perfect order. Flowers on every table and lovely, longing, sad-looking rooms.

I've never liked a single photograph. If you hate it here I'll help you find an apartment, but I hope you won't. And next spring maybe you can help me look for a house — in the country. It's past time. I don't want to live in the city. I've not found myself in the catalogues.

In the winter I tell myself I have to be here for the shop, but I need a summer place where I can get away. Only I'm chicken. I want land but I see myself buying a lush seven acres and with my care watching it turn to burning desert all around me. Within weeks.

Analysis: *Brontosaurus*

Type: Seriocomic
Synopsis and Character Description
Note: The role of the Antiques Dealer can be played by either a man or a woman.

The action of the play takes place in present-day New York City. The play opens with the Antiques Dealer waiting for the arrival of his/her nephew. The Dealer, late forties, is extremely verbose and relating to his/her assistant the plot to the movie *The Little Shop of Horrors.* The Dealer explains to the assistant how, much like the plant, s/he's looking for someone to "feed me, sustain me, make me believe." S/he doesn't mention anything about being a killer like the infamous Audrey 2.

The Dealer's sister says that the Nephew is a puppy dog. S/he's just happy to have someone around to talk to all the time although s/he's pretty sure s/he'll turn the young boy homosexual.

The Dealer refers to her/himself as myopic, filled with an enormous hope that is general and vast and unspecific. S/he is also extremely verbose, almost never stops talking, like a speed freak. While s/he may be along in years, s/he's a moral adolescent.

The Nephew is four hours late and the Dealer is very worried. Dealer dismisses the assistant, there is a jump in time, and suddenly the Nephew is there. The Dealer's verbal assault begins immediately, and s/he tells the Nephew not to be scared, s/he's all protective coloring: a facade.

The Dealer drinks Manhattans and asks the Nephew to fix one, but the Nephew doesn't know what that is. The Nephew, here to study theology at NYU, is a threatening, almost dangerous presence whose entire being is the opposite of the Dealer's. The Dealer admits s/he can't even keep a plant alive.

Time passes. The Dealer and the Nephew cohabitate, but as strangers. The Dealer can't get them to eat or spend any time together, and it drives him/her crazy. The two finally have some time together and the Nephew recounts the moment in which he knew he had to become a minister. The Nephew then explains he's leaving to go live with friends and he had never intended on staying. The Nephew leaves, and the Dealer realizes s/he will be alone forever.

Given Circumstances

Who are they? The Dealer is talking to his seventeen-year-old nephew.

Where are they? The Dealer's NYC apartment.

When does this take place? The present.

Why are they there? The Nephew is staying here while he attends college.

What is the pre-beat? The Dealer asked if the Nephew's Methodist parents drink alcohol.

Questions

1. Can you state your objective in a simple, specific, and active way?
2. Who are you talking to? Be specific and have a clear image.
3. Can you think of three adjectives to describe your character?
4. Did you ever want children of your own?
5. Are you excited about having your nephew here with you?

6. What is his name?
7. What does he look like?
8. Does he make you nervous?
9. Where in New York is your apartment?
10. Is your shop in the same building?
11. How big is your business?
12. How much money do you make a year?
13. What do you enjoy most about antiques?
14. Do you drink a lot?
15. When is the last time you saw your sister?

Women's Monologues

Stanton's Garage
Joan Ackermann

LEE

Do you know how many people count on me? How much? Count on me with their lives? He . . . that's . . . I took two days off from work to drive his daughter to his best friend's wedding. I organized his plane ticket.

I had his suit drycleaned, picked it up, dropped off his dogs at the kennel, drove him to the airport. I bought and mailed the wedding present he doesn't even know what it is.

What an asshole! Excuse me. Is that an asshole? Is he an asshole?

I am engaged to this person. I'm supposed to marry this person in two months? Why? Can you tell me why? I was sitting in the car trying to figure out if I really deserved to feel as bad as I was feeling and I started to wonder why someone like me, a woman who has been through med school, who has spent years—in my residency, in my practice, in the hospital— years combating, successfully, the enormous, colossal egos of male doctors, why would I put myself in a relationship with a man who does nothing but put me down? Does it make sense? Does it make sense to you?

You know, this year . . . this year . . . has been so strange, I can't tell you. I have lost my nerve, lost it. I've had these . . . fears, these unspecific, low-grade, chronic fears I don't know what they're rooted in. I used to be so tough, you can't imagine, on top of everything. I can't explain it.

Analysis: *Stanton's Garage*

Type: Dramatic
Synopsis

The action takes place in a small service station in upstate Missouri. It's the only garage for thirty miles.

Silvio, Harlan, and Denny—a motley, well-meaning crew—all work here. Today they're dealing with the broken-down cars of Lee and Ron. Both are on their way to the same wedding, but they don't know it, or each other. The wedding is in the town of St. Joseph. The owner of the garage is in Mexico, so it's very difficult to get a straight answer from anyone about cost, repair specifics, or time. Ron's car gets fixed and he leaves. Harlan, seventeen years old, thinks the problem with Lee's car might be the fuel injectors. When Harlan says he has to drive somewhere to get new injectors, Frannie offers to go with him. Frannie is the sixteen-year-old daughter of Lee's boyfriend. Frannie says she can pick up food on the trip, and she secretly tells Harlan that she'll pierce his ear when they get back.

In actuality, no one at the garage knows how to fix the car. Lee misses the wedding luncheon, then cocktails. Frannie starts pumping gas for customers to kill the time. The staff tells Lee she might need a whole new computer system. After seven hours, Lee finally breaks down and calls Henry, her boyfriend, who is furious with her. He yells at her and hangs up.

Ron appears late at night, with a black eye. Lee, who's sleeping in the garage, thinks it's a burglar and she shoots at him, breaking a $1,000 bottle of wine. Ron says the black eye is from Harry, who was bad-mouthing Lee at the wedding. Ron came to her defense. Morning comes and Lee tells Frannie she's going back to Chicago and leaving Harry. Frannie tells Lee she kissed her first boy, Harlan. The ladies find the Volvo manual, fix the car themselves, and drive home.

Character Description
Lee, 40

Lee is from Chicago. She's travelling with Frannie, sixteen years old, her fiancé Harry's daughter. The car broke down and Lee is mad at herself because both Harry and his ex-wife told her to have the car serviced before taking the trip and she didn't. Harry is the best man at the wedding, and Lee is supposed to play piano for the ceremony. Lee calls the wedding venue but specifically asks not to talk to Harry—she just has someone relay the message that she is running late. The car broke down after Lee stopped it when Frannie wanted to look at a deer in a field. Frannie is a city kid, so she doesn't see sights like that often.

Lee is a doctor. She was previously married, but her husband died after a long illness. She used to go rock-climbing with her husband. She says she used to be very brave. Now she's afraid all the time and she doesn't know why.

She took two days off from work for the wedding as well as organized Harry's plane ticket, had his suit dry cleaned, arranged the present, etc.

Given Circumstances
Who are they? Ron and Lee met briefly early yesterday.

Where are they? Stanton's Garage in upstate Missouri.

When does this take place? The present, 2:00 a.m.

Why are they there? Lee's car broke down. Ron is returning from crashing his ex-wife's wedding.

What is the pre-beat? Ron tells Lee that Harry told everyone at the wedding that he can't count on her.

Questions

1. Can you state your objective in a simple, specific, and active way?
2. Who are you talking to? Be specific and have a clear image.
3. Can you think of three adjectives to describe your character?
4. How long were you married to your first husband?
5. He died five years ago. Do you think about him every day?
6. How did you and Harry meet?
7. Did he remind you of your first husband?
8. Do you love Harry?
9. What are the signs that things are going wrong?
10. What does Frannie look like?
11. Do you love her?
12. When are you and Harry getting married?
13. What does Ron look like?
14. Do you find him attractive?
15. When did you lose yourself?

Sondra
Laura Cahill

BARB

What do you think of the house? Nice, isn't it?

I told you. I'm planning on renovating it, you know? It has good bones. It's older than all the houses in the vicinity because they were all built in the years after.

Yeah, yeah. People always say, "Barb, you have an old house," it's like they've never seen anything old before. Everyone wants something new, but I'm not like that. When my husband was around he did a few things to fix it up, but that was a long time ago. He says "I'm coming over, I want to finish that project," and I say, "Alright, we're waiting," and he never shows up. Thanks, but no thanks, Stan.

I think he is crazy. I think you're right there, Joe. You wouldn't believe how he treated me. I have real stories. I'll tell you some time. We'll sit down and have a drink and I'll tell you all of it.

He didn't want to leave, but he had to. His girlfriend stabbed him in his car. She made him move in with her.

Analysis: *Sondra*

Type: Seriocomic
Synopsis

The action of the play takes place in working-class New Jersey. It's a town dense in population, intersected by highways, and just out of reach of anything special. It's the kind of place that would make anyone feel stuck.

Sondra is nineteen years old. She lives with Barb, her mother, in an old house at the end of a lonely street. It's also the kind of place that would make anyone feel stuck. Sondra works at the mall. She's the assistant manager of accessories at JCPenney, but she has plans to get out—out of this house and out of this town. Barb isn't going anywhere. She's a cocktail waitress, most likely born and raised in this town. She's divorced and on a manhunt. Barb has taken in a boarder for the spare bedroom, a working man named Joe. Joe works at Auto Parts Express on Route 9. He's also an assistant manager. Joe takes an instant liking to Sondra, not Barb.

Barb is constantly trying to make money. Joe is a way to get more money in the house. She also has a side business in which she sells watches designed to "align your electric currents preventing negative takeover." In essence, scam watches that are supposed to prevent cancer. Joe asks Sondra out, leaves her notes, and becomes an uncomfortable and dangerous presence in the house for Sondra. Barb is unaware of this and won't listen to Sondra when Sondra asks for help.

Jennifer is Sondra's on-again/off-again best friend. Most of her peers find Sondra strange. She writes in her journal all the time. She's not man-crazy. She has dreams of getting out. Most people in this town dream of getting through the week so they can party all weekend. Jennifer is pregnant again and about to get an abortion. Sondra is stable, so Jennifer has gravitated toward her.

Joe keeps making advances on Sondra that she keeps dodging or rejecting. Joe begins to sell watches for Barb and invites Bucky over to make a sale. They end up just hanging out and drinking with the girls. Jennifer takes an immediate interest in Bucky, because he's a man. They play a game called "truth or lie" and Sondra gets very drunk. Jennifer goes for a ride with Bucky, leaving Joe and Sondra alone. Joe confronts Sondra about being stuck up. In the final scene, Barb returns home from work to find Joe packing and leaving and Sondra gone. Jennifer returns without Bucky and sits on the stoop with Barb as they wait for Sondra. They're not aware of Joe's anger or intense feelings for Sondra.

Character Description
Barb, 40s
Barb is a cocktail waitress and probably has been for quite some time. Her daughter is nineteen years old. Barb tries to better her life, by renovating the house, taking in a tenant for extra money, and selling the eco-watches. She is, however, not the most organized person. She drinks a glass of wine every night before her shift while putting on her makeup. She keeps a bottle of vodka under the sink and doesn't like the girls drinking from it. The clock in the kitchen works, but it's permanently wrong, so you have to subtract two hours and add ten minutes, math she does on her fingers whenever she's looking for the time. The kitchen cabinets are filled with past-dated food. She eats mostly fast food.

Given Circumstances
Who are they? Joe is Barb's new tenant.

Where are they? The kitchen of Barb's house.

When does this take place? The present.

Why are they there? It's morning and Joe is getting ready to go to work.

What is the pre-beat? Joe thanks Barb for making him coffee.

Questions

1. Can you state your objective in a simple, specific, and active way?
2. Who are you talking to? Be specific and have a clear image.
3. Can you think of three adjectives to describe your character?
4. What's Joe's most attractive feature?
5. Did you put makeup on before coming down this morning?
6. What happened between you and your husband?
7. How much money do you make as a cocktail waitress?
8. Were you actively looking for a tenant before meeting Joe?
9. Where did you meet Joe?
10. How does it make you feel to have a nineteen-year-old daughter?
11. What do you see when you looks in the mirror?
12. Is this what you expected your life to be like?
13. When you were a kid, what did you dream you'd be?
14. Did you ever want to get out of New Jersey?
15. Do you think Joe will save you?

Poetic License
Jack Canfora

DIANE

I'm sorry?

Well, you're a wily one, Edmund, you've caught us. They were actually written by Sir Francis Bacon . . . no, wait—Kevin Bacon . . . no, not Kevin Bacon, but someone who knows him—

You're not joking. You're really . . . oh, Edmund . . . please . . . don't. Don't turn out to be crazy. If you think somehow that . . . (*a realization*) are you one of those people? Oh God, you're one of those people, aren't you? You're one of those people who think it's not enough to read the novels or poems or whatever . . . like the one who waited outside Bob Dylan's house every night to comb through his garbage cans—it's sick. And people like that focus so much on the minutiae they can't possibly see the overall picture clearly. Which means that inevitably they get even the basic things terribly wrong. Which is OK within limits; I mean that's why God invented graduate schools, based on what you've just said to me, I think maybe you're a garbage picker. Or it's worse than that—you're an academic. Not that I should bite the hand that gags me, but . . . you're one of those sad people who goes around . . . dusting the language for fingerprints.

My God, living with my daughter—Poor Katherine's going to have to take an ambulance to therapy.

OK, OK, let's take this a step at a . . . why would you say something like that? Because John is different from his poems?

Of course he's different from his poems. That's why he wrote them down. That's why it's a talent—a skill, to make poetry of things. To concentrate feeling like that. That's why the poets always disappoint. At least the ones who don't kill themselves.

Analysis: *Poetic License*

Type: Seriocomic
Synopsis

"Every family's a foreign country. Impossible to understand all the nuances of the native culture."

Katherine Greer and Edmund, her poet boyfriend, come home to her parents' very upscale and sophisticated house. They are to celebrate the birthday of Katherine's father, John. Katherine is nervous about Edmund meeting her parents. The couple has just moved in together but plan on keeping that fact a secret. Edmund is nervous about meeting John, as he's a genius writer with a Pulitzer Prize. Katherine reassures him that he's not the one to worry about. Both Katherine and Edmund are writers.

John's life is pretty much run by his wife, Diane, and that worries Katherine. She feels like Diane, her mother, overextends him. John and Diane are waiting to get confirmation about him being named poet laureate. They're remaining tight-lipped about it until it's official.

Diane has managed to turn the birthday into a media circus with a PBS special in the works, among other things. Katherine refers to it as "a reality show for English majors." The tension between Diane and Katherine rises, and the way they battle over John makes everyone uncomfortable. Edmund drops a veiled, unspecific threat on John when the women leave the room.

The call about his selection as poet laureate comes through, and Diane springs into action. One of the reasons she wanted Katherine here this weekend is because she knew this might happen, which makes Katherine furious. She storms off, and John goes to comfort her. Edmund confronts Diane with the issue at hand. He believes that a woman named Zora Gibson wrote all of John's initial work. Zora was Edmund's mother. He accuses John of stealing her poems. Edmund wants John to admit this publically and co-credit Zora. John admits to using Zora's words as inspiration, as much as he's used anyone's words for inspiration. He will not admit he stole anything. This ambiguity, and Edmund's betrayal, throws Katherine into a tailspin of doubt.

The media shows up and Edmund leaves, but he has given Katherine all of Zora's papers that prove his case.

Character Description
Diane Greer, 40s
Katherine says Diane's "charm offensive" is "like Amanda Wingfield on a coke binge." She is educated and open-minded, and tries to treat her daughter like an adult. She uses her husband's status as a Pulitzer Prize winner to get dinner reservations at restaurants. She books lectures for him. She makes him write essays. Diane manages John. She sweeps into a room rather than merely entering, whether there's an audience or not. Tells Katherine immediately that she's too skinny. Almost immediately attempts to guilt Katherine for not telling them more about Edmund. These big, important events make Diane nervous, but she also thrives off of them. Diane calls out the fact that they're living together without telling her. She went to grad school. She listens to a lot of NPR.

Given Circumstances

Who are they? Edmund is Katherine's new boyfriend.

Where are they? The living room of Diane and John's NYC apartment.

When does this take place? The present.

Why are they there? It is John's birthday.

What is the pre-beat? Edmund stated that John hasn't written his poems.

Questions

1. Can you state your objective in a simple, specific, and active way?
2. Who are you talking to? Be specific and have a clear image.
3. Can you think of three adjectives to describe your character?
4. What was your initial impression of Edmund?
5. Prior to this moment, does he make a good match for Katherine?
6. How long have you and John been together?
7. Are you happily married?
8. Do you still love him?
9. What do you find most attractive about him?
10. Would be be successful without you?
11. Do you like John's poetry?
12. What did you go to school for?
13. Can you define your life outside of your relationship to John?
14. Who does your daughter look like?
15. Is there any truth to Edmund's accusation?

Place Setting
Jack Canfora

ANDREA

I've had a week to digest it. I wasn't this calm about it at first. And I'd suspected something was up for a while. Months. Before he was even conscious of it, I think.

Greg will come back here. He will. I'd say within the hour. He'll be tempted to go—he'll want to go—but in the end, he'll stop just short. My guess is he's telling her that right now. I'm . . . when you get married, Lenny, with whomever it may be, when you do—you have to—figure out what's of value to you. What's most important. It's maybe tougher to figure out than you realize. Hang on to that. And then everything else has to be negotiable. Otherwise . . . it'll all go. People wonder what Greg and I have in common—and it's not much but it's good enough. It's this—

Greg will come back because he knows—he will believe— he's obliged to. He will come back and he'll stay. And not only will I accept that . . . I'm very moved by it.

He will come back to me even though what he wants most in the world is to run away. How could you ever want more than that from a person?

I'm very happy to be married, but at the same time, I've found it—very humbling. Because . . . inevitably there's this— moment when you—you catch yourself looking at him with . . . disappointment. Not over anything he's done—that would be better, because then there would be something to *fix*—but simply because . . . you *know* him. You know him as well as you can know a person—and that's always enough to break your heart. And then it hits you—*he* must have moments when he looks at *you* with that same disappointment. That's a . . . tough corner to turn. But you decide what matters to you and . . . you compromise.

He'll come back—that's his compromise. And I'll take him back without him ever knowing I knew. That's mine.

Analysis: *Place Setting*

Type: Dramatic
Synopsis

The action of the play takes place in Greg and Andrea Idleman's suburban New Jersey home on New Year's Eve 1999. The home is modest but nice. The other couples at the celebration are Laura (Andrea's younger sister) and Richard, her filmmaker boyfriend, and Lenny (Greg's older brother) and his girlfriend Charlotte.

Andrea prepared an amazing meal to celebrate the millennium. Greg has been glued to the TV all day watching New Year's Eve celebrations in other countries for signs of Y2K breakdowns. Although more guests are expected later, Andrea wanted to do a quiet dinner with family first. There is visible tension between Andrea and Laura when Laura brings up their alcoholic mother. There's also tension when Lenny grills Richard on his filmmaking ambitions. Richard wants to make a documentary about Ulysses Grant being gay, even though it's only a theory; he has no evidence to back it up.

Canfora is deftly examining the various stages of relationships. Andrea and Greg have been married for years. Lenny and Charlotte have been together for a few years and are approaching the time when marriage becomes a possibility. Laura and Richard have just started dating. Charlotte and Greg are having an emotional affair that is quickly leading to more intimate acts—they have a heated sensual encounter in the kitchen while everyone else is in the other room. Then Lenny comes in and proposes to Charlotte. Laura and Richard get into a huge fight and try to leave before midnight, sparking a fight between Andrea and Laura. Charlotte confesses her love to Greg and they kiss just before midnight.

The next morning Andrea reveals the affair to Lenny. She's known for a week, having found a letter Charlotte wrote to Greg. Lenny confronts Greg. Their relationship is destroyed. Andrea is faced with the realization of what the rest of her life will be like.

Character Description
Andrea, early 40s

Andrea is practical and somewhat conservative. She is a great cook and even decorated the house for New Year's Eve. Andrea and Greg were going to go to Paris on their honeymoon but she talked him into a trip to Hawaii instead. Greg is an ad writer but still writes creatively in his free time. Andrea thinks Greg's writing is very good but she's biased. When Laura tells Andrea she's getting a tattoo, Andrea dismissively calls them a trend. She wanted to have a small dinner with family before other people came over. She's protective of Greg, especially around Richard because he's an artist doing what he set out to do and Greg, to some extent, settled for stability. She doesn't like when anyone else tries to do something in the kitchen, such as clean up or load the dishwasher, because they won't do it right. She's been very emotional lately but hasn't shown it. She's pregnant and just told Greg.

Given Circumstances

Who are they? Lenny is Greg's older brother.

Where are they? The kitchen of Andrea and Greg's suburban home.

When does this take place? New Year's Eve and New Year's Day, 1999.

Why are they there? Greg and Andrea threw a dinner party for the holiday.

What is the pre-beat? Andrea has just told Lenny about Greg's affair with Charlotte.

Questions

1. Can you state your objective in a simple, specific, and active way?
2. Who are you talking to? Be specific and have a clear image.
3. Can you think of three adjectives to describe your character?
4. How long have you and Greg been a couple?
5. Do you still love him?
6. What is his most attractive feature?
7. What is his most annoying habit?
8. Did you have any suspicions about his affair?
9. How long have you know Charlotte?
10. What does she look like?
11. Do you think of you and Charlotte as equals?
12. What does Greg write about?
13. Have you put as much energy into your relationship as you have into your home?
14. What did you study in school?
15. Are you looking forward to having a baby?

The Road Down the Mountain
Jack Canfora

JULIE

This is the mystery of you, Tom. Well, not mystery, it's pretty common, actually, the glib, cynical ones are usually recovering sentimentalists, but it's still a shock to hear it.

You still want art to mean that much. And before Adam's accident, you'd have maybe gotten me to agree with you, in a, in a, theoretical way. But ultimately, when you're helping the man you loved—the man you'd hitched your life to—when you're helping him take a bath or clean himself after you get him off of the toilet because he'll never be able to do that on his own again, that sort of pious adolescent shit just sounds embarrassing.

Maybe all the people who think they have an intimate relationship with him should help take turns feeding and bathing and wiping him for the next few decades. And psychotically enough, some of them probably would. Because they're so addicted to the fantasy of being *understood* and *understanding*. But it was all a fantasy to begin with. And now even the shadow of that fantasy's gone. They didn't know him, not really, they, they didn't go for walks with him down the mountain.

We had moments where . . . no one will ever know about them. Only the two of us. And now he's, he's gone. Only I remember. And it's . . . so we'll do this interview and you'll see the shell of Adam's former self and then, hopefully, they'll, you'll—everyone will leave us all alone.

Frankly the notion of me being able to brainwash Adam's disrespectful to the man they're supposed to be so worshipful of. He was a grown man; he did what he wanted.

All I did was open him up to new experiences.

Analysis: *The Road Down the Mountain*

Type: Dramatic
Synopsis

The action of the play takes place in Julie and Adam's home in the Teton Mountains of Wyoming. The house is so beautiful and expansive that it almost feels like a ski lodge. Tom, a reporter who specializes in music, comes to the home to interview Julie about Adam, a famous musician. Adam and Julie dropped off the radar five years ago. Two years ago Adam was in a car crash, and the extent of his physical injuries isn't known to anyone but Julie and Corey, their assistant.

Tom thinks Adam's music is very important/significant, but he has gone into seclusion at the height of his fame, so his overall contribution to the industry remains to be seen.

Tom hasn't had an article published in about two years. This opportunity is very high-stakes for him. There is a mythology surrounding Adam. His first album was released almost twenty years ago, and all three of his albums are still in the top 100.

Julie is doing this interview after five years of silence because the media won't let up. She hopes doing this one means they will finally leave them alone. Julie admits that Adam suffered severe spinal and head injuries, he'll probably never walk again, and he's not the man she married.

The interview is as much about Julie and Tom, the end of their relationship, and their lives since that event as it is about Adam. Julie calls off the interview. Corey intercepts Tom and tells her he'll have a story. She gives him an album of songs that Adam wrote for Julie before the accident. Julie had no idea it existed and only finds out after Tom interviews Adam.

Character Description
Julie, 40s

Julie and Tom go back a long way. They used to be a couple. She invited him here because she trusts him. She doesn't trust many people, especially reporters. Julie hasn't made an appearance in public in over five years. She hasn't made this decision to talk lightly. Julie likes to control what's controllable. She chose Tom for this because he needs it and he will be somewhat beholden to her for choosing him. She isn't very good at interviews. She prefers the days when she was a blogger and could walk down the streets unnoticed. She isn't sure why everyone in the press hates her but assumes it's because she's a woman and she married a very talented, successful man. Julie and Corey are in a relationship despite Corey being a woman and much younger.

Given Circumstances

Who are they? Tom is there for an interview. He and Julie used to be lovers.

Where are they? Julie and Adam's home in the Teton Mountains, Wyoming.

When does this take place? Winter 2015.

Why are they there? Tom has come to interview the couple for a magazine article.

What is the pre-beat? Tom is trying to sell Julie on the importance of the interview.

Questions

1. Can you state your objective in a simple, specific, and active way?
2. Who are you talking to? Be specific and have a clear image.
3. Can you think of three adjectives to describe your character?
4. How coherent is Adam since the accident?
5. How has your relationship changed since the accident?
6. Are you lonely?
7. Do you miss the person Adam used to be?
8. Do you miss the life you used to have?
9. Do you miss Adam making new music?
10. What feelings has Tom returning brought up?
11. Has Tom changed since you last saw him?
12. Why did your relationship with Tom end?
13. Have you thought about him much since it ended?
14. What does protecting Adam consist of?
15. How often do you listen to the album of songs about you that Adam recorded?

Burnt Orange
Lila Feinberg

JANE

We were just discussing this old Fender. I'm afraid we're selling it. But that's the beauty of antiques—they can begin their life anew no matter how old they get. Wish that was true about middle-aged women!

You came home late last night . . .

That's okay—I'm sure Hunter didn't mind too much. Oh how I miss those late city nights! I used to go clubbing with my girlfriends til dawn. Everybody would always tell us that we didn't have a care in the world. But you know? I had just escaped from my little hick town in Pennsylvania, ran off to a commune, then to the city. I was away from my family for the first time in my life . . . I think I must have been wild out of fear of being anything else. That's the funny thing about being a girl. You're terrified of so much of the world, and yet you look back and realize how much gumption you had in you. If only you had known it then. Or rather, known what to do with it.

I saw your mom yesterday . . . .

She said she's tried calling you several times since you got here—

I told her things were working out wonderfully. And that you were such a lovely young lady.

I know you're busy dear, but she would love to hear from you. Even just your voice.

Well, I'm off to a long day at the clinic.

Analysis: *Burnt Orange*

Type: Dramatic
Synopsis

The play takes place in a doorman building on the Upper East Side. Avery shows up with a mountain of baggage. She's not moving in, she's "migrating." Avery is coming to Jane's apartment but is greeted by Hunter, Jane's son. Apparently Jane has sublet his room without letting him know. Avery has already paid $1,000 for the month, so she has to stay; that was all the money she had.

While Avery gets the rest of his stuff, Hunter confronts his mother. She says they need the money and he promised he was going to return to school this year. Hunter asks why she didn't ask his father, and Jane explains that his new wife won't allow it now that they are expecting a baby. Avery finds some journals and newspaper clippings in a drawer that pique her interest.

Harrison, her hedge-fund non-boyfriend, wants to spend more time with her, but he's picked up cues from her that say back off. He's set up an oxygen-controlled tent in his bedroom. Avery has a panic attack in the tent during sex and leaves.

Avery has a dream about Nate, Jane's young son who's in the journals and the clippings. She wakes up when her bed collapses. Hunter helps her screw the bed together. He asks Avery if she ever gets sick of playing some role—something she thinks she should be. Avery answers, "No that's the thing—I think we only ever get sick of playing ourselves." Hunter tells Avery that the room she's staying in used to be his brother Nate's. Hunter found him dead at fifteen. Avery gathers her stuff and goes even though Hunter insists that she stay.

Avery's mom has a serious accident. After spending a week in the hospital with her mother, Avery returns to the apartment. The ghost of Nate begins appearing to Avery, not just in dreams, but all the time. Avery breaks up with the hedge-fund boyfriend, makes peace with Hunter, and goes off into the world; maybe she goes home for once.

Character Description
Jane, 40s

Jane is an ex-hippie. She now works as an acupuncturist. Her fifteen-year-old son Nate died recently of a drug overdose. Her older son, Hunter, has left college and is living back at home with her. In an effort to try and move on, Jane has rented Nate's room to Avery, the daughter of a patient. They have a dog, a pit bull named Bob Marley. Jane seems constantly exhausted and frazzled. She has untamed hair and wears loose, new-agey clothing. She did nothing to prepare the room for Avery, including telling Hunter that someone was coming. There are boxes of Nate's belongings that need to be donated; she just hasn't had a chance to do it. She wants Hunter to go back to school. Jane is divorced and her ex has remarried. Jane has an active, engaging mind and is taking classes currently to learn more about acupuncture.

Given Circumstances

Who are they? Avery is renting the room of Jane's deceased son.

Where are they? The living room of Jane's Upper East Side apartment.

When does this take place? The present, 7:30 a.m.

Why are they there? Jane is taking pictures of Nate's guitar in order to sell it online.

What is the pre-beat? Hunter has just stormed out of the room.

Questions

1. Can you state your objective in a simple, specific, and active way?
2. Who are you talking to? Be specific and have a clear image.
3. Can you think of three adjectives to describe your character?
4. In what ways were you a hippie?
5. How long were you and your husband married?
6. How long have you been divorced?
7. Did you have a good/close relationship with Nate?
8. Did you know he was using drugs?
9. What was your relationship with Hunter like before Nate's death?
10. Has it changed? How so?
11. If Hunter goes back to school, what will it be like in the apartment?
12. Is it difficult getting rid of Nate's belongings?
13. What is it like having Avery in the apartment?
14. How does it make you feel that Avery is avoiding her mother?
15. What interests you about acupuncture?

Recall
Eliza Clark

JUSTINE

You know who I will not miss? Ed.

Lucy, come here and watch this show with me. You ever see this show?

Okay, so that guy, he used to weigh four hundred and thirty pounds which means he weighed about as much as a brown bear. A small brown bear, but I mean, a freaking bear. And that lady with the mole, she used to weigh three hundred pounds. They said that's like a record for someone that small—I mean, for fuck's sake, she's practically a midget. Four foot six and a half, they said. Anyhow, they're the final two 'cause they lost the most weight. Now they have to run a mile carrying all the weight they lost in chicken fat.

Well, 'course it's gross, that's the idea. It's like a deterrent. Like spraying a dog with lemon—it's like these people need to know that if they get that fat again, walking around is like dragging three hundred pounds of chicken fat everywhere you go.

Ed was a deadbeat. Ed had a fat ass and a bad temper and the man was no expert in the bedroom.

You don't worry about me, okay? I'll find a new Ed, no problem.

Analysis: *Recall*

Type: Seriocomic
Synopsis

Justine sits in a motel and watches TV. She delivers this monologue while her daughter, Lucy, who is in her early teens, scrubs a human-sized bloodstain off the floor. This action is an immediate clue to the audience that something is not right in their world. Justine and Lucy now have to leave town. Lucy feels like she was just beginning to fit in and make friends, but there's no way around it. They can't tell anyone they're leaving, including Lucy's teachers. They are just going to pack up their few belongings and go.

Lucy and Justine are taken to a safe house. There they meet David, who takes care of them and makes them comfortable. He awkwardly flirts with Justine, and Lucy notices it immediately. We learn that people are after Lucy, but we don't know why. David does this work because he wants to protect the innocent. He carries a gun for safety.

When Lucy can't sleep, she asks her mom to "erase her memory." With a few words a few beeping noises, Justine does this and Lucy sleeps. Whether this is real or psychological we don't know, but it works in getting Lucy to sleep.

Lucy goes to a new school where she meets Quinn, a boy her age. She's getting "tested" by the school nurse. It's never stated what for. She's now calling herself Tiffany. Quinn says there's literally nothing to do in this town. Quinn lets on that he has a violent streak. Lucy seems to have one, too, and it's implied that perhaps she's the one who killed Ed.

David buys sandwiches for the ladies and an early birthday cake for Lucy. This makes Justine cry. David really likes Justine.

The punishment for the kids' acts of violence is getting "fish-tanked" and monitored by doctors and scientists. Quinn and Lucy are just two of many. Meanwhile we learn that Justine's sister, Charlotte, is the one who assigned David to their case.

As David and Justine's relationship progresses, Lucy realizes that her mom is always the one who reveals too much. Justine's neediness gets the better of them and destroys their safety. Justine has figured out that David works for the system that could take Lucy away from her forever. She asks him just to let her know when they're coming for them so she has time to get Lucy and run. Lucy tells Justine it's time to go again. Charlotte gets her hands on Quinn and puts him in the fish tank; she freezes him until they find a cure for the disease. The play ends with Justine erasing Lucy's memory in another motel in another city.

Character Description
Justine, 40s
Justine has a teenage daughter, Lucy. She won't eat after 7:00 p.m. because she doesn't want to gain weight. She watches reality weight-loss shows, like *The Biggest Loser*. She says, "a woman's ass is one of her treasures." So she can't get fat. Justine used to be a singer in a band. David says she seems likable, but Justine refers to herself as a "pain in the ass." She has a sister, but they don't talk. The sister possibly works for the government. She irons with very few clothes on to get David's attention. She gets scared of Lucy. Justine refers to Lucy's dad as "Dirty Steve." She refers to herself as "spunky."

Given Circumstances
Who are they? Lucy is Justine's teenage daughter.

Where are they? A cheap motel room.

When does this take place? The present, or the not-too-distant future.

Why are they there? Justine and Lucy are constantly on the run.

What is the pre-beat? Lucy has just killed Ed.

Questions

1. Can you state your objective in a simple, specific, and active way?
2. Who are you talking to? Be specific and have a clear image.
3. Can you think of three adjectives to describe your character?
4. What did Ed look like?
5. How long were you seeing him?
6. What about him did you find attractive?
7. How did he make you feel?
8. Was he something special, or a distraction?
9. How did he die?
10. Are you scared of Lucy?
11. Do you love her?
12. How long have you two been on the run?
13. How do you pay the bills?
14. What does she look like?
15. Do you resent her at all?

God Gave Us Aunts
Idris Goodwin

AUNT KELLY

I've got something to show you.

Don't be shy. Come on. But be quiet. Your mama's asleep.
We don't want to wake her up.

(Pats around for something. Finds it—a folded 8 × 10 sheet of paper.)

This is for you. It's a list.
I wanna give this to you—but I have to kind of explain it to you first.
I see how your mother talks to you and don't get me wrong.
She is my sister and everything but—Don't get me wrong.

But I don't see a little girl
when I see you. I see a young woman. Yeah—an older girl.

You are a . . . a viper, like your Aunt Kelly. And these are all the things you gotta know.

1. *Everybody is going to tell you what they know, but nobody knows—except your Aunt Kelly.*
2. *That movie The Bodyguard is a lie. Nobody is coming to save you.*
3.

Looks like I crossed that one out.

What is that?

Oh, (*chuckles into her hand*) stupid Frank wrote this. Such a—Why don't we just save 3 until your 18th birthday?

4. *Your friends are not your friends.*
5. *It's going to hurt the first time. It's always going to hurt the first time.*
6. *But it gets better, for a while at least, until it gets worse.*

Your mom and dad take you to church and they'll teach you about thy neighbors and love and thy and don't and do. That's—great—that's positive but positive is overrated.

7. *Positivity is something losers who don't know that they're losers say when crap is hitting the fan.*
8. *Learn how to cook—but not for that reason.*
9. *The monsters and wolves in your fairy book are real—*

I wouldn't tell you this if it wasn't true. This is why you have an aunt. Your mom and dad, they can't tell you this stuff. It's against the rules I guess. I was 18 before I knew it, and my aunt, your great aunt Sandra—she waited until I was 18 to give me my list but it was kinda too late. So I'm saying it to you now, what're you now, 11? Oh, really? Just 9, huh? Oh, you look so much older.

Analysis: *God Gave Us Aunts*

Type: Seriocomic
Synopsis and Character Description

This piece was written as a stand-alone monologue, so all of the factual information you need about the character and events can be found within.

Aunt Kelly is in her forties. She is speaking to her nine-year-old niece, giving her some life philosophy because she received all of this information too late in life. It's up to you to decide exactly what that means. Did she get married too young? Did she have a baby too soon? Or drop out of school and give up her dreams?

Aunt Kelly sees something in this little girl/young woman that reminds her of herself at that age. She calls her a "viper." A viper is a venomous snake that has long fangs that it uses to inject its poison. What is it about this young girl that makes Aunt Kelly think she needs this information? Aunt Kelly says it's because of the way her sister, the child's mother, talks to the girl. Aunt Kelly sees this young girl becoming a woman, a fierce woman, and so she shouldn't be spoken to like a child because she needs to learn how to protect herself.

Aunt Kelly's list is filled with information that points to the fact that life is disappointing and hurtful. People, both strangers and friends, can and will hurt you. And yet the sharing of this list means that Aunt Kelly is still filled with love and hope. Although it seems like life gave up on her, she hasn't given up on life.

When crafting this list you, the actor, need to come up with a really specific scenario that occurred in Aunt Kelly's life that triggered these realizations. Each and every disappointment/lesson came from a specific incident. Craft those incidents and personalize them for yourself.

You need to know what number 3 is and why she doesn't share it.

Is Aunt Kelly the older or the younger sister? How does that affect her relationship with her sister and this child?

It's important to know and understand the journey a forty-something African American woman went through to get where she is in America today, especially a woman like Aunt Kelly, who appears to have had few privileges.

Given Circumstances

Who are they? Aunt Kelly is talking to her young niece.

Where are they? It's not specified in the script. Aunt Kelly's house? Her sister's house?

When does this take place? The present.

Why are they there? It's not specified in the script. Aunt Kelly is visiting? Babysitting?

What is the pre-beat? It's up to you to decide.

Questions

1. Can you state your objective in a simple, specific, and active way?
2. Who are you talking to? Be specific and have a clear image.
3. Can you think of three adjectives to describe your character?
4. What is your niece's name?
5. Does she remind you of yourself at that age?
6. How did you go about creating this list?
7. How did you learn each and every one of these lessons?
8. What does your sister look like?
9. Has she had a better/easier/more successful life than you?
10. Are you married?
11. Do you have children?
12. Did you want children?
13. How do you maintain your positive attitude?
14. Why did you cross out number three? What does it say?
15. What does it mean to be a "viper"?

The Tutor
Allan Havis

MRS. BENTLEY

You know my husband had climbed Mount Everest last spring. He spent over sixty-five thousand dollars to reach the summit. Never asked me if I would object.

He trained for three months. I told him that 1 out of eleven assholes die at Everest. "What's death?" said hubby. George loved the odds because he's an asshole. His life insurance strictly forbade extreme sports like sky diving and Vegas orgies. Had George died, no payment to the beneficiaries. Worse, Orson was really upset like an infant wetting his bed at night — wicked dreams about Everest. George bundled his vacation time — independent to us — to make this his own little triumph. He read *Into Thin Air* — you know, books on tape — and was obsessed like a pimpled face boy scout. My mother told me to file for divorce, but George met his goal. He reached the summit under ideal conditions. Dumb luck.

All this became his bragging rights even though George was one of the forty guys who passed a dying British climber. David Sharp. It was in the newspapers, of course. "Dilettantes from a dozen countries and their underpaid sherpas turn their back to Brit climber!"

I screamed at George when he told me the news, but all he said was that's the mountain code. "You focus on your goal. Period." (*Pause*) Like Orson, I had a lot of weird dreams when George was away. I really believed he was going to die a horrible death or come home crippled. And if truth be told, I wanted him to come back a paraplegic. Did you ever see that film *Breaking The Waves* with Emily Watson? (*Pause*) Since he came back from Everest, George feels totally invincible.

Analysis: *The Tutor*

Type: Seriocomic
Synopsis

The play opens with the very first tutoring session between Seth Kane, the tutor, and Orson Bentley. Seth has been hired to help Orson with his work in English class. The first novel on their list to discuss is *The Great Gatsby* by F. Scott Fitzgerald. Orson is aggressive, reactive, and assaultive. He tries desperately to get a rise out of his new tutor. Seth deftly handles everything Orson throws at him.

Seth prefers working with troubled teens. Currently, he teaches in the public school system. Orson's father is a skilled businessman and has negotiated Seth's fee for this work down to a pittance. Mr. Bentley has also revealed to Seth that he and his wife are on a trial separation and he is already seeing someone in his office because he needs "magic" in his life. Seth finds himself on the receiving end of Mrs. Bentley's depression and sexual advances. In fact, the entire family seems to be taking advantage of him in one way or another.

Despite the tension and dysfunction, Seth keeps returning. His relationship with Orson seems to be developing and helping the boy. The Bentley house is broken into, and pieces from Mr. Bentley's gun collection go missing. Seth speaks with a young woman claiming to be Orson's girlfriend. She says that she is pregnant with Orson's baby and that he is obsessed with Columbine, feeling a kinship with Dylan Klebold, one of the gunmen. Seth presses Orson to admit whether or not he's planning a school shooting, but Orson is so coy and such a skilled liar that Seth can't decipher fact from fiction.

Orson and Tucker, his best friend, kidnap someone from school. Orson calls Seth and asks him to come and take him home. It turns out that Orson acted alone. There is no Tucker. Orson crafted the entire scenario. When Seth discovers this, he terminates his relationship with Orson and then mysteriously ends up in the hospital in a coma. Was Orson the cause of this coma?

Character Description
Mrs. Bentley, 40s

Her full name is Madeline Bentley. She's attractive and well educated, both qualities that helped her land a successful, attractive husband. She has to have a drink every night around 6:00 p.m. because she can't stomach the news when she's sober. She believes herself to be a very good wife. She has a very dry sense of humor and tells Seth that's the best way to get through to Orson. She believes Orson has turned a corner and is on the road to being better. She believes hormones were the cause of his bad/erratic behavior. She seems almost relieved when she learns of her husband's affair. Her facial muscles relax for the first time in years. She did sign a prenup before marrying. She's a pop culture aficionado.

Given Circumstances

Who are they? Seth Kane is Orson's new tutor.

Where are they? The living room of the Bentley home in Southern California.

When does this take place? 2006.

Why are they there? Seth is waiting for Orson.

What is the pre-beat? Mrs. Bentley just quoted Ogden Nash and asked Seth if he happened to be related to the writer.

Questions

1. Can you state your objective in a simple, specific, and active way?
2. Who are you talking to? Be specific and have a clear image.
3. Can you think of three adjectives to describe your character?
4. Is your home well appointed?
5. How much care did you take in decorating the home?
6. What does Seth look like?
7. Are you attracted to him?
8. How do you feel about your husband's affair?
9. How long have you been married?
10. Were you ever in love with Mr. Bentley?
11. What does Orson look like?
12. Are you worried about him and his future?
13. What is your alcohol of choice?
14. If you start drinking at 6:00 p.m., what time do you stop?
15. How will you support yourself if you get divorced?

The Tutor
Allan Havis

MRS. BENTLEY

Orson was lucky. He nearly killed a homeless man at a city intersection.

Orson is wired differently from other boys. Maybe he's just like his father. Neither George nor Orson have any sense of remorse about their actions. They only believe in luck.

You would think they have stones in their heart. They must be reptilian. And as a result they don't feel deep hurt of others. But they damn know the distinction between right and wrong. They know how to argue for the underdog. And they always win. If they are wrong, they make it right. Because words are full of tricks.

I don't expect you to instruct Orson on ethics and moral behavior, because you might as well teach a monkey to sing. Well, actually I saw a monkey sing on Animal Planet cable and I was very impressed.

Is this all crazy talk? I must be very lonely, Mister Kane. And that's worse than ovarian cancer.

Of course, George thinks I'm sleeping with you at Motel Six. High style adultery. And what the hell can I say about that?

Analysis: *The Tutor*

Type: Dramatic
Synopsis

The play opens with the very first tutoring session between Seth Kane, the tutor, and Orson Bentley. Seth has been hired to help Orson with his work in English class. The first novel on their list to discuss is *The Great Gatsby* by F. Scott Fitzgerald. Orson is aggressive, reactive, and assaultive. He tries desperately to get a rise out of his new tutor. Seth deftly handles everything Orson throws at him.

Seth prefers working with troubled teens. Currently, he teaches in the public school system. Orson's father is a skilled businessman and has negotiated Seth's fee for this work down to a pittance. Mr. Bentley has also revealed to Seth that he and his wife are on a trial separation and he is already seeing someone in his office because he needs "magic" in his life. Seth finds himself on the receiving end of Mrs. Bentley's depression and sexual advances. In fact, the entire family seems to be taking advantage of him in one way or another.

Despite the tension and dysfunction, Seth keeps returning. His relationship with Orson seems to be developing and helping the boy. The Bentley house is broken into, and pieces from Mr. Bentley's gun collection go missing. Seth speaks with a young woman claiming to be Orson's girlfriend. She says that she is pregnant with Orson's baby and that he is obsessed with Columbine, feeling a kinship with Dylan Klebold, one of the gunmen. Seth presses Orson to admit whether or not he's planning a school shooting, but Orson is so coy and such a skilled liar that Seth can't decipher fact from fiction.

Orson and Tucker, his best friend, kidnap someone from school. Orson calls Seth and asks him to come and take him home. It turns out that Orson acted alone. There is no Tucker. Orson crafted the entire scenario. When Seth discovers this, he terminates his relationship with Orson and then mysteriously ends up in the hospital in a coma. Was Orson the cause of this coma?

Character Description
Madeline Bentley, 40s

Madeline Bentley is attractive and well educated, both qualities that helped her land a successful, attractive husband. She has to have a drink every night around 6:00 p.m. because she can't stomach the news when she's sober. She believes herself to be a very good wife. She has a very dry sense of humor and tells Seth that's the best way to get through to Orson. She believes Orson has turned a corner and is on the road to being better. She believes hormones were the cause of his bad/erratic behavior. She seems almost relieved when she learns of her husband's affair. Her facial muscles relax for the first time in years. She did sign a prenup before marrying. She's a pop culture aficionado.

Given Circumstances

Who are they? Seth Kane is Orson's new tutor.
Where are they? The living room of the Bentley home in Southern California.
When does this take place? 2006.
Why are they there? Seth is waiting for Orson.
What is the pre-beat? Seth asked her about Orson's hit and run.

Questions

1. Can you state your objective in a simple, specific, and active way?
2. Who are you talking to? Be specific and have a clear image.
3. Can you think of three adjectives to describe your character?
4. Is your home well appointed?

5. How much care did you take in decorating the home?
6. What does Seth look like?
7. Are you attracted to him?
8. How do you feel about your husband's affair?
9. How long have you been married?
10. Were you ever in love with Mr. Bentley?
11. What does Orson look like?
12. What other kinds of trouble has he gotten into?
13. What is your alcohol of choice?
14. If you start drinking at 6:00 p.m., what time do you stop?
15. How would you support yourself if you get divorced?

Death Tax
Lucas Hnath

TINA

I do have a kid. Yes.
And he is in Haiti.
And I am here.
But that's all you know.
Is that all you know?

That is all you know.
And you've made up, in your head, a whole story about it.
But whatever I tell you, you'll tell yourself is a lie.
My word against—who knows what.
Well. Here.
Here's something I can show you.

That's him.
That's John Paul.
Alright.
You see he's real.
He's 8 years old.
And he's real.
And
I dunno, what can I tell you—
He likes to swim.
He swims fast.
And . . . he also likes diving.
He wants to be on a diving team.

He does well in school.
He's one of the smartest in his class.
He is maybe number 2 or 3 in his class—he's very smart.
He reads lots of books.
He's read the entire Bible.
He memorizes whole pieces from the Bible.
And someday, he wants to be either a doctor
or a preacher.
And he acts like a little adult sometimes.
He has very serious eyes.
My husband and I, we would fight.
And he would try to talk to us.
He would try to make the fight stop,
he would try to work it out.
That's the type of kid he is.
Wise beyond his years. Kind of weird.
And I look at him,
and I ask myself how did I make that?
How did that come from me?
He is the best thing I ever made.
There is no reason,
no reason, I should have made him.
Because I *was*,
I *was* bad.
When I was young.
I'm different now.
I've changed.
But when I was young,
I was a bad girl.

Analysis: *Death Tax*

Type: **Dramatic**
Synopsis

The action of the play takes place in a nursing home in December 2010. Maxine, an elderly woman, near death and very wealthy, is a patient. Tina, a Haitian nurse, takes care of her. One day during a routine vitals check Maxine says to Tina, "I know that you are killing me." Tina denies this accusation.

Maxine has her shut and lock the door. Maxine explains that the tax laws are changing on the first of January. At that point the amount of money her daughter will receive upon Maxine's death with decrease substantially. Maxine believes that her daughter, knowing Tina makes very little money, offered her an incentive to speed-up her death.

Maxine says her daughter has already asked for, demanded the money, before Maxine's death. Maxine explains she can't change her will at this point.

Maxine knows that Tina has a child in Haiti whom she would like to bring to America. Obviously Tina's job, income, security and well-being are all at stake with this accusation.

Tina finally says that the daughter is going to pay her $1,000 to kill Maxine and another $1,000 when it's done. We don't know if Tina is telling the truth or just trying to get through the situation. Maxine offers her $1,000 for every week she stays alive. If Maxine makes it to January 1 she'll give Tina an additional $200,000.

Tina goes to Todd's office and asks for a leave of absence. Now that she has money she needs to quickly work with lawyers to get her son here. Todd and Tina were lovers. He tells her that another nurse (Nurse Toad) has seen her taking a check from Maxine. This is against policy. Tina points out that this nurse has made false accusations before and they are documented. Tina tells Todd about her deal with

Maxine. If Todd can help keep Maxine alive until January 1, then Tina will split the money with him.

Maxine's daughter shows up, but Maxine won't see her. We learn that the daughter is on food stamps and has a young son. She desperately needs money now, but her mother won't even see her. The daughter knows, from Maxine's lawyer, that checks are being written every week—sizable checks—and to whom the money is going. The daughter has had a document drawn up saying she will give up all rights to Maxine's money if she can just see her. She asks Tina to give the papers to Maxine. Todd tells Tina she can't get involved and everything has to stay the way it is.

The action jumps twenty years into the future and Maxine is still alive. She is running out of money and the home is discharging her, but she has nowhere to go and few options. Charley, her grandson, comes but refuses to take her in or pay for her health care. He is mad at Maxine for the way she treated his mother, her daughter. He leaves, and Maxine is left to face her future, her death, alone.

Character Description
Tina, early 40s

Tina is a nurse in a nursing home. She is Haitian and speaks with an accent. She is responsible for taking patients' blood pressure, checking for signs of swelling, and monitoring their vital signs. Tina is practical and efficient. She is also very bright. She makes little money at the nursing home and needs all she can to bring her eight-year-old boy, John Paul, here with her. When her son was born she realized she had been living a bad life and became a Christian. Her husband did not change, so she divorced him, but they share custody. One weekend he had their son and did not come back. No one in authority would help her. And her husband said if she comes back to Haiti and tries to get John Paul, she will pay. Tina and Todd were lovers. She still uses sex, or the promise of it, to manipulate him when necessary.

Given Circumstances

Who are they? Maxine is Tina's patient.

Where are they? Maxine's private room.

When does this take place? December 2010.

Why are they there? Maxine has no one to care for her but does have a lot of money.

What is the pre-beat? Maxine suggests Tina would take money from Maxine's daughter to kill her so that Tina could bring her son here from Haiti.

Questions

1. Can you state your objective in a simple, specific, and active way?
2. Who are you talking to? Be specific and have a clear image.
3. Can you think of three adjectives to describe your character?
4. What has your relationship with Maxine been like up until this point?
5. What ailments does Maxine suffer from?
6. What does taking care of her, physically, include?
7. When is the last time you saw John Paul?
8. When is the last time you talked to him?
9. What was your life in Haiti like?
10. How is life here better? Worse?
11. What are your living arrangements?
12. How much money do you make a year?
13. How much money do you need to get John Paul?
14. Have you taken money from Maxine's daughter to kill her?
15. Are you scared you'll lose your job?

While You Lie
Sam Holcroft

HELEN

Amy's teacher called; I had to pick her up. They said she was 'assaulting' her classmates.

They very firmly said, 'She cannot go around *assaulting* her classmates like that.' Climbing on their backs.

It's all right, I sorted it out. I told her what she saw was a boy dog asserting itself over a girl dog. I explained that it's only the boys that do the asserting, not the girls.

And so then she asks why, and I said because they are animals. And animals don't have equality between the sexes.

Don't worry, I explained it to her in terms she could understand: we are not dogs. We *used* to live like dogs, we *used* to walk on our hands and eat raw meat and carry our children in our mouths. And men used to climb on the backs of women and because there was no shelter, no running water, no heat, and they had to keep order to survive. But, gradually, as time went by, we began to walk upright, and eat with our hands and we learnt to speak. Now we have supermarkets full of food and central heating and cinemas and men don't need to assert themselves any more because they are civilized.

I said, 'Why don't you ask your daddy? He'll tell you he has no need to assert himself in this day and age.'

Analysis: *While You Lie*

Type: Dramatic
Synopsis

The plays begins in the bedroom of Ana and Edward. They are forty minutes late for a party, but Ana is still undecided about what to wear. The two fight. Edward says, "I long to be honest with you but you're so sensitive that I have to watch everything I say." Ana says the relationship is over and kicks him out. Ana is very insecure. She lives in England, but she is a foreigner. She wants to be successful but lacks the confidence in herself necessary to succeed.

In the next scene we see Ana at work, wearing Edward's shirt. Chris is her boss and Ana, his secretary. She's demanding a raise and suggests that sex might be in the cards if he obliges. Meanwhile Chris has a child and a pregnant wife, Helen, at home.

Ana goes home and packs up Edward's things. He comes to collect them and they have yet another argument, this one about Ana sleeping with Chris. Edward goes to Chris's home—he had been there at a barbecue the previous summer—to confront Chris. Helen is home alone and Edward finds himself unable to do it. He makes a sexual advance on Helen and she rejects him.

As Ana and Chris's affair escalates, Helen begins to suspect something. She goes to a plastic surgeon to research several surgical options that will keep her looking young, fit, and beautiful. She plans on paying for this with the money Chris gave her to remodel the kitchen.

Amy, Helen and Chris's five-year-old daughter, begins acting up at school. Helen feels the pressure of solo parenting coupled with Chris's affair pulling her apart.

While You Lie is a brilliant dissection of two relationships and how one action can affect many people. Holcroft also shows our ability to be one thing with someone and then totally different with another. He explores the various forms of humiliation we go through put others through, both willingly and unknowingly. Holcroft also demonstrates how far someone will go to be seen in their relationship.

Character Description
Helen, early 40s
Helen is married to Chris, pregnant with his child, and raising Amy, their five-year-old daughter. Their home is spacious, expensive, and well-kept. Helen has recently sensed a shift in her marriage, but she's not certain what exactly is going on. Their large home makes them responsible for community gatherings. They have a summer barbecue every year. People expect this and depend on them. They have upward of 150 guests there, and it's also a celebration of Helen's birthday. When Chris isn't in the room, Helen rifles through his jacket and pockets looking for receipts.

She goes to a plastic surgeon and considers multiple surgeries to keep herself attractive for her husband. Although she's pregnant, she starts to eat baby food out of a small bowl in an effort to control her weight.

Given Circumstances
Who are they? Helen and Chris are married.
Where are they? The kitchen of their home.
When does this take place? The present.
Why are they there? Chris is getting home from work, late.
What is the pre-beat? Chris is trying to cut back costs on Helen's birthday party.

Questions

1. Can you state your objective in a simple, specific, and active way?
2. Who are you talking to? Be specific and have a clear image.
3. Can you think of three adjectives to describe your character?
4. How long have you and Chris been a couple? Married?
5. What is his most attractive feature?
6. Do you still love him?
7. Are you happy/excited about the new baby?
8. Are you hoping the baby is a boy, or a girl?
9. How big of a family do you want?
10. Is Chris's success important to you?
11. Do you like having money?
12. Is it important to you to own nice things?
13. Have you ever had an affair?
14. What more do you want from your life at the moment?
15. What are you really saying to Chris with this monologue?

The Whale
Samuel D. Hunter

MARY

She's — awful, isn't she?

Ellie. She's awful. She's a terror.

Charlie, she doesn't have any *friends*. Not a single one. She's so cruel that no one at school will even *talk* to her.

When she was nine, ten, I thought — I'm not giving him the satisfaction. I'm not letting him see this awful little girl and blame it all on me. No way.

But later on — when she was fifteen, sixteen. I was worried she would hurt you. You've been around her for two days now, and already she's almost killed you.

I was protecting you, Charlie. You've always been so fucking sensitive, ready to break down over anything . . . And here's this girl — this girl who takes *pleasure* in hurting people, this *terrible* girl.

Believe me Charlie, I don't take any pleasure in admitting it, I'm her mother for Christ's sake. I spent way too many years saying to myself, she's just rebellious, she's just difficult. Charlie — she's evil.

Analysis: *The Whale*

Type: Dramatic
Synopsis

The action takes place in Charlie's apartment in northern Idaho. Charlie weighs 600 pounds. He never leaves the apartment. He teaches online classes on expository writing. In the midst of masturbating to gay porn, Charlie begins to have trouble breathing. Simultaneously, there's a knock on the door and in pops a Mormon missionary. Charlie has the young man call Liz, his friend and caretaker, but refuses medical treatment.

Charlie has no health insurance and won't go to the hospital. Liz tries to get Elder Thomas, the missionary, to leave because she has issues with the Mormon Church. Liz tells Charlie that if he doesn't go to the hospital he will die before the week is out. He has congestive heart failure. Liz doesn't want Charlie to die—he's her only friend. But still she brings him a bucket of fried chicken.

Charlie, knowing the end of his life might be near, calls his daughter Ellie. Ellie is seventeen years old and a senior in high school. Ellie doesn't tell her mother, Mary, that she's going to see her father. Charlie and Mary haven't seen each other in fifteen years. Charlie offers Ellie money to stay with him and also assistance in writing essays for school. Ellie comes over but doesn't really engage with Charlie. He tells her he won't force her to be there. She'll still get his money and he'll still write her essays, but he does want to get to know her. Ellie starts to interrogate Charlie. He reveals that he put on all the weight when his partner, Alan, died. Alan was the son of a Mormon bishop. His father asked him to come to one more service and Alan did, against Charlie's wishes, and from that point on his health deteriorated until he died. Charlie never found out what was said at that service.

Charlie's health rapidly deteriorates day by day. He wants to know that Ellie will be taken care of once he dies, not just financially, but spiritually and emotionally. Mary comes over to see him but offers no reassurance on those points. Liz is furious when she learns of Charlie's secret savings, because she thinks he should have been using that money to save his life. Everyone in this play is looking for a home, a safe port.

Character Description
Mary, early to mid-40s

Mary is Charlie's ex-wife and the mother of Mary, seventeen years old. She doesn't want Ellie seeing Charlie. Ellie says she's happy when she drinks. Mary finds out from her friend Judy that Ellie is seeing Charlie. She makes Ellie promise to stop visiting. She does ask how much weight Charlie has gained. Mary doesn't like talking about Charlie. She smokes. Mary and Charlie had a deal to give Ellie the money once she was grown and out of the house. Charlie says she's cynical. She's not working at the moment. She fought Charlie really hard in court for full custody of Ellie, and won. Mary feels bad for never acknowledging Alan's death.

Given Circumstances

Who are they? Mary and Charlie were formerly married and have a seventeen-year-old daughter.

Where are they? Charlie's apartment in Idaho.

When does this take place? The present.

Why are they there? Mary found out Ellie has been visiting Charlie against her wishes.

What is the pre-beat? Charlie asks if it's so awful that Ellie has a gay father.

Questions

1. Can you state your objective in a simple, specific, and active way?
2. Who are you talking to? Be specific and have a clear image.
3. Can you think of three adjectives to describe your character?
4. What did Charlie look like when you married?
5. What does he look like now at 600 pounds?
6. How does it feel to see him after fifteen years?
7. Were you really in love with him?
8. Did you think the two of you would live together forever?
9. Have you had a serious relationship since Charlie?
10. Were you looking forward to being a mother?
11. Who does Ellie look like?
12. Why have you kept her from seeing Charlie all these years?
13. Are you looking forward to her going away to college?
14. What did you think your life would be like at this age?
15. Do you love your daughter?

Strike-Slip
Naomi Iizuka

VIVIANA

What are you doing with that?

That's your father's gun.

You going somewhere?

Don't lie. Don't lie to me. What do you need that for? Protection? You think that's going to protect you? You really think that, huh? You have no idea. *No sabes nada.*

You think I don't understand? I understand more than you will ever know. I've been down this road already with your father. I'm not going down it again.

Before you were born, you had a hole in your heart. They showed me pictures of you, when you were inside of me. They were all gray and blurry, like those pictures you see from outer space, like photographs of some far off galaxy. I thought you were going to die. That's what the doctors said. But you didn't die, and I thought it was a kind of miracle.

Sometimes I think it would have been better if you had. It would've been better than watching you throw your life away like a piece of garbage.

You walk out that door now and you don't need to come back. That's it.

Analysis: *Strike-Slip*

Type: Dramatic
Synopsis

A strike-slip is a fault rupture in which pieces of ground move parallel to each other, causing vibrations or shaking.

The play opens in a small market in downtown Los Angeles. Richmond has come in to buy some smokes and lottery tickets. Lee, the Korean owner, gives Richmond change. Richmond says he paid with a ten and a five. Lee says it was a ten and one. The two argue and Richmond leaves with a threatening, "I'll be back."

Lee is the father of Angie. Richmond appears to be plotting something with Vince, to take revenge on Lee. Rafael's mother, Viviana, is a real estate agent and she's about to sell a very expensive home to a Caucasian couple, Dan and Rachel, in Santa Monica. Iizuka slowly unfolds a world in which race, status, and finances dictate how people experience the American Dream.

No one is happy in this world. Viviane wants her son to grow up and be a successful businessman, unlike his father. Dan is having an affair with Vince. Richmond feels oppressed and disrespected.

Angie tries to steal money from her father's store to leave town, and he finds her. He slaps her repeatedly. Vince comes in and offers her money. She refuses him. Viviana finds Rafael packing his gun. She tells him if he takes it to never come back. Someone comes into the market and Lee shoots. Lee ends up in prison for shooting and killing someone.

Vince is in business with Richmond and has been skimming merchandise off the top for himself. Richmond knows this.

Rafael and Angie move in together. She is pregnant. Richmond ropes Rafael into his business. Rachel hits Angie in a car accident.

Everyone is connected one way or another, our every move has an effect.

Character Description

Viviana Ramos, 40s

Viviana is Mexican American, first-generation American, born and raised in Los Angeles. She is a real estate agent who lives in Highland Park. Rafael is her son. She has worked hard and has big dreams for him to become a successful businessman or a lawyer. She can feel him slipping away.

Given Circumstances

Who are they? Rafael is Viviana's son.

Where are they? Viviana's Highland Park, Los Angeles home.

When does this take place? The present.

Why are they there? Viviana has just come home from work. She finds Rafael packing.

What is the pre-beat? Viviana finds Rafael holding a gun.

Questions

1. Can you state your objective in a simple, specific, and active way?
2. Who are you talking to? Be specific and have a clear image.
3. Can you think of three adjectives to describe your character?
4. What's your favorite memory about Rafael's father?
5. How quickly have the last seventeen years gone?
6. Do you see Rafael's dad when you look at your son?
7. What path do you wish your son had taken?
8. How long have you been in real estate?
9. Do you like your job?
10. Is it what you always wanted to do with your life?

11. How much money do you make a year?

12. Are you comfortable? Successful?

13. Have you ever threatened your son like this before?

14. Do you know/like his girlfriend?

15. Where do you see yourself in five years? Ten? Twenty?

Appropriate
Branden Jacobs-Jenkins

TONI

Bo, I just had the crap scared out of me by a teenybopper banging around my dead father's kitchen and now you're telling me Frank is here, that Frank the family pedophile is here and that he is upstairs?

What is he doing here?

Is this really happening? Where was he at Dad's funeral? Wait—Did he know we were here!?

Where has this bastard even been for the last—how many— Oh my god, has it been ten years? Has it been a decade, Bo? Why would he—Oh my god, he's here for—Is Frank here for money? Oh my god, he's here for money! Are you—I literally cannot believe this is happening—I'm going to have a panic attack—I'm going to kill him!—

We have to get him out of here, Bo!

Analysis: *Appropriate*

Type: Dramatic
Synopsis

It is summer in the South and the cicadas are everywhere. A family has converged on this small rundown property because their father, Ray, has recently passed. It's up to the children to pack up, sell, or throw out the years of stuff inside and unload the house. This was formerly the family's summer house, but Ray moved into it permanently years ago. As is the case with most high-staked situations like this, fights break out often and they're mean. The return of Frank, the black sheep of the family, now calling himself Franz, towing along a seemingly underage fiancée, doesn't help matters. This family defines dysfunction.

The estate is half a million dollars in debt. Toni plans on having an auction but has — severely, in her brother Bo's eyes — mishandled everything. In fact, because of Toni, the sale of the house might put them even further in the red. The house is a major liability and a difficult sell because there's an old family cemetery on the property.

As the family cleans out the house, horrible things are found. Ainsley finds a photo album filled with photos of lynchings. Cassidy and Rhys discover jars of body parts in the study. Was Ray a racist and a murderer, or a collector of ephemera?

Although they try to hide the album from their children, everyone sees it. No one succeeds in throwing it out, because it may be worth money. Franz, in a fury, and in an attempt to cleanse himself and his family, runs into the lake with the photos, pretty much destroying them.

Character Description
Toni, early 40s

Ray's daughter, sister of Bo, mother of Rhys. The family grew up in D.C. She lives in Atlanta now, divorced from Derek. Rhys plans on leaving his mom and living with his father for the summer, which is breaking her heart.

Toni and Bo had decided on liquidators to handle the estate, but Toni fired them, saying they were too expensive. Instead she hired people from Craigslist to handle the sale. While Bo financed their father's life and death, Toni dealt with the practicalities and actual hands-on maintenance. Bo calls her a control freak. Toni curses a lot.

She believes her father had nothing to do with the photos. He was a good man. After Rachael's monologue recounting Ray's reference to her as Bo's "Jew wife," Toni "jokingly" calls Rachael a "shylock" and a "kike." Bo calls Toni a terrorist.

She used to be principal at a school but was fired when Rhys was discovered selling drugs.

Given Circumstances

Who are they? Bo is Toni's brother, and Rachael is his wife.

Where are they? The living room of a former plantation home in Arkansas.

When does this take place? The present, summer.

Why are they there? Toni's father has just died, and the family is there to pack up and sell the house.

What is the pre-beat? Frank, Toni's other brother, has appeared unexpectedly and uninvited with his fiancée.

Questions

1. Can you state your objective in a simple, specific, and active way?
2. Who are you talking to? Be specific and have a clear image.
3. Can you think of three adjectives to describe your character?
4. How hot is it here?
5. How long have you been here?
6. How long ago did your father die?
7. Did you love him?
8. What were the practical details of taking care of your dad at the end of his life?
9. Do you miss him?

10. Do you resent Bo for being successful and living far away?

11. What does Rhys look like?

12. Do you feel like you're losing him, too?

13. When is the last time you saw Frank?

14. Do you think he's really a pedophile?

15. Do you think of yourself as racist?

Appropriate
Branden Jacobs-Jenkins

RACHAEL

You want to look at the way he treated me?

Ray obviously had real problems with me because of my heritage and this . . . anti-Semitism was always very uncomfortable for Bo and I . . . So I don't think his . . . race issues are so far of a leap.

First of all, I did not call him an anti-Semite. He was in possession of anti-Semitic traits. Anti-Semitic traits like wh- Like having a problem with Jews, Toni!

I don't have to prove anything to you.

I once overheard your father referring to me as Bo's "Jew wife." We were visiting him the summer I was pregnant with Cassidy and he was on the phone and he didn't know I was standing there and I overheard him refer to me as "Bo's Jew wife." "Bo and his Jew wife are here from New York." Now would someone like to explain to me why it was necessary to distinguish to whoever this person was that I was, in fact, a Jew?

Why couldn't I just be Bo's wife?

And that's just a small example. Your father had a very difficult time with me and the fact that I was Jewish, which is maybe why he was very distant to me and Bo and our kids. And did I feel the need to say anything to him? No. He was an old man. You can't blame people for the ways they were raised . . . And I don't expect you guys to be totally . . . be able to grasp this, because you've never been discriminated against, but that's how it is.

Analysis: *Appropriate*

Type: Dramatic
Synopsis

It is summer in the South and the cicadas are everywhere. A family has converged on this small rundown property because their father, Ray, has recently passed. It's up to the children to pack up, sell, or throw out the years of stuff inside and unload the house. This was formerly the family's summer house, but Ray moved into it permanently years ago. As is the case with most high-staked situations like this, fights break out often and they're mean. The return of Frank, the black sheep of the family, now calling himself Franz, towing along a seemingly underage fiancée, doesn't help matters. This family defines dysfunction.

The estate is half a million dollars in debt. Toni plans on having an auction but has—severely, in her brother Bo's eyes—mishandled everything. In fact, because of Toni, the sale of the house might put them even further in the red. The house is a major liability and a difficult sell because there's an old family cemetery on the property.

As the family cleans out the house, horrible things are found. Ainsley finds a photo album filled with photos of lynchings. Cassidy and Rhys discover jars of body parts in the study. Was Ray a racist and a murderer or a collector of ephemera?

Although they try to hide the album from their children, everyone sees it. No one succeeds in throwing it out because it may be worth money. Franz, in a fury, and in an attempt to cleanse himself and his family, runs into the lake with the photos, pretty much destroying them.

Character Description
Rachael, 40s

Rachael is married to Bo. They have two children, Ainsely and Cassidy. It was Rachael's idea for everyone to stay together at the house: the kids could experience some of their father's childhood, and they never really got to know their grandfather.

This is the first stop of the summer. After they clear up the estate, the family is going to do a long trip home through the South and see some of America. Usually they do Europe in the summer, but money is tight this year. Rachael doesn't want anyone cursing in front of Ainsley, which is difficult with Toni around. She also doesn't want Cassidy spending any time alone with Rhys. She says that Toni is turning Rhys gay and that he is warped like all the men in the family are.

She is Jewish and the family she married into is not. How much she practices her faith is not clear.

Given Circumstances

Who are they? Bo is Rachael's husband and Toni is her sister-in-law.
Where are they? The living room of a former plantation home in Arkansas.
When does this take place? The present, summer.
Why are they there? Bo's father has just died and the family is there to pack up and sell the house.
What is the pre-beat? The family has recently found the photos, but Toni doesn't want to hear anything about her father's alleged "issues."

Questions

1. Can you state your objective in a simple, specific, and active way?
2. Who are you talking to? Be specific and have a clear image.
3. Can you think of three adjectives to describe your character?
4. Do you think your father-in-law was racist?
5. Do you think Toni is racist?
6. Do you believe these photos belong to your father-in-law?
7. How terrible were the photos?
8. Do you believe you're more evolved than Toni?
9. Have you and Toni always crossed swords?
10. Does this information cause you to question your husband and his beliefs?
11. Why haven't you taken your daughter and left?
12. Are money and status important to you?
13. Are you resentful that you're here instead of in Europe?
14. How are things between you and Bo at the moment?
15. How are things with you and your children?

The Veri**on Play
Lisa Kron

CAROL

Nine months? Is that what you call a long time? Try seven years. You just wait till you've been fighting with the phone company for seven years!

They say I'm dead.

(*She pauses for effect.*)

Do I look dead to you?

My father died, seven years ago. I sent the phone company a copy of his death certificate to close his account. Would you like to see the letter they sent me in return?

(*Pulls out a crumpled form letter and reads.*)

"Dear Ms. Anderson. Our sincerest condolences on the recent death of Carol K. Anderson."

They cut off my phone service *seven years ago* and they still won't turn it back on because according to them *I'm dead*!

(*Her rage turns to grief.*)

I go there in person, I stand by the payment windows, I scream: *I'm alive! Look at me! I'm alive!!!*

Nothing makes a difference. Nothing helps. Seven years! Seven goddamn years!!!

Let me tell you something, Janey. These people, these brave people are the only thing that gives me hope.

Thank you.

Analysis: *The Veri**on Play*

Type: Comedic
Synopsis

Jenni, a smart, hip, young aspiring professional, finds herself falling down the rabbit hole of billing nightmare with a phone company called Ferizon. In this epically funny play, Lisa Kron dissects not only the dangers of customer service, but the cost of keeping up with trends and the power of technology in today's culture.

A misplaced payment of $153.64 takes over ten months to get processed correctly. Once Jenni tells her story, everyone she meets shares an equivalent (or worse!) tale of customer service woe. Numerous calls to Ferizon, which we see acted out, result in nothing. Jenni finally thinks the situation has been taken care of until one day she receives a call from Ferizon telling her she has an outstanding balance. Jenni comes close to having a breakdown.

She attends a support meeting for a group called PHBICS or "People Hurt Badly By Inadequate Customer Service." It's there that she hears the stories of Lars and Carol and realizes she is not alone. The group meets in a shabby, nondescript East Village tenement building. The meetings are high-stakes and stressful, and result in arguments. It's actually the opposite of what a support group should be.

Jenni receives a call from Ferizon telling her that her service will be cut off for lack of payment. It is. Jenni has a breakdown. She can't go on. She swears she will live without phone service. Some people from PHBICS take her to the Port Authority to show her what waits out there in the rest of the world—worse customer service.

The play ends with an anti-Ferizon musical number. Jenni's phone service gets restored—only to relay to her that she must call Ferizon customer service. We can't escape them. There's no way out. They run the world.

Character Description

Carol, 40s

Carol is an old-school, cranky New York lady.

Carol speaks to the point. She often says what everyone else is thinking, no matter the consequences. She has no filter. She wants everything to function on time. She can be quite passive-aggressive when she doesn't get her way. No one has it worse off than her. No one has worked harder than her. No one knows her pain and struggle.

Given Circumstances

Who are they? A meeting of PHBICS.

Where are they? An ungentrified East Village apartment building.

When does this take place? The present.

Why are they there? It's a support group.

What is the pre-beat? Jenni says her problem with Ferizon has been going on for nine months.

Questions

1. Can you state your objective in a simple, specific, and active way?
2. Who are you talking to? Be specific and have a clear image.
3. Can you think of three adjectives to describe your character?
4. How long have you been coming to these meetings?
5. How many people have you seen come and go in that time?
6. Whose customer-service issues have been worse than yours?
7. Why do you continue to come here every week?
8. What's your point of view on Jenni?
9. Do you think her problems will get solved?
10. Do you care?
11. Why are the people in this group "brave"?

12. How have you managed without a phone for seven years?
13. Who would you call if you had a phone?
14. What does "old-school, cranky New Yorker" mean?
15. What do you do for a living?

The Method Gun
Kirk Lynn and Rude Mechs

ELIZABETH

I hate my voice.

I hate the way my voice sounds.

I hate the way my voice sounds when I'm inside the theater
building.

I hate the way my voice feels in my throat.

I hate the way my voice makes my body jiggle like jello.

I hate my ears.

I hate my odd-shaped ears.

I hate it when he hugs me and his face is right beside one of
my ears.

I hate my face.

I hate the way my face looks in stage make-up.

I hate the way my face looks when I laugh.

I hate laughing onstage.

Hahahahahahahahahaha.

I never know what to do with my hands.

I hate my hair.

One day rehearsal was nothing but noticing how often I blink.

I'm surprised I see anything.

I like dancing.

I like to sit and listen to music on stage.

You can hear a song one hundred times in your apartment
but on stage everything is completely transformed.

You take a normal woman from my hometown

put her on stage and play her a song
and if she listens closely
that song will be transformed into the most beautiful song in
 the world.
And the woman will be transformed, too.
Her ears will grow huge
and her face will contort
and her hands will fly around her body like wounded birds.
I asked Stella why it doesn't happen the other way.
Why doesn't the woman grow perfect and live forever?
And Stella wrote out an explanation for me
and put it in this box and locked it
and gave me the key
and told me whenever I wanted to know the answer
I should unlock the box and open it
and take out the letter
and light it on fire
and read as much of it as I can before it burns out.

Analysis: *The Method Gun*

Type: Seriocomic
Synopsis

The Stella Burden Company's production of Tennessee Williams's
A Streetcar Named Desire has been in rehearsal for nine years. Stella
"left" her company (and students) on August 26, 1972. Stella was a
revered teacher, director, and force in the American theater throughout
the 1960s and 1970s. She walked out on her company, immigrating
to South America, never to be heard from again and giving no reason
for her departure.

For nine years her company of actors have been rehearsing *Streetcar*, but without the characters of Stanley, Stella, Mitch, and Blanche—the main characters. All the students have are "artifacts" left behind by Stella, including a gun that was loaded promptly upon her departure but never fired. Stella always kept a loaded gun in the rehearsal room to "remind us that we can kill each other, or her, or ourselves, I guess."

Throughout the course of the play, the company demonstrates some of the Burden training technique such as "Crying Practice," during which they must cry for three minutes straight.

During the play, which is really more about relationships than events, the actors perform exercises, recreate scenes from the nine-year rehearsal process, and show us scenes from before Stella's departure. They reveal that Stella had devised this *Streetcar* as a way of teaching them how to play small roles. One student theorizes that she left because none of them learned a single thing she was trying to impart.

Character Description
Elizabeth, 40s
Her full name is Elizabeth Jones. She's been rehearsing the role of Eunice in *Streetcar* for the past nine years. She believes that the students are straying from "The Approach" as laid out to them by Stella Burden. She suffers from major panic attacks. She lets Rob hold her when she's upset but threatens that she's going to tell the company about his drinking problem. Mostly, she doesn't want to fight with Rob anymore.

She's been proposed to at least one time.

When Stella doesn't show up, Elizabeth comes up with the idea to sell all of the studio equipment and move the company to Mexico, continuing their study there.

Given Circumstances

Who are they? Elizabeth is elaborating on a filmstrip titled "What Makes an Actor."

Where are they? A theater and rehearsal space.

When does this take place? This particular piece takes place in July 1975.

Why are they there? It's twelve days before the opening of *Streetcar*.

What is the pre-beat? This monologue is the entire scene.

Questions

1. Can you state your objective in a simple, specific, and active way?
2. Who are you talking to? Be specific and have a clear image.
3. Can you think of three adjectives to describe your character?
4. How many actors are in the company?
5. Who are you closest to? Furthest away from?
6. How does it make you feel to give your opinion about theater?
7. What did you learn from Stella?
8. What is your theory on where Stella went?
9. Are you sorry your relationship with Robert is over?
10. What do you love most about acting? Hate most?
11. How do you support yourself?
12. What character do you feel closest to in *Streetcar*?
13. Does it bother you that you're not getting the chance to play Blanche?
14. Has being in rehearsal for such a long time been frustrating?
15. What would make this process/production successful in your eyes?

Bad Habits
Terrence McNally

DOLLY

Our wedding night was terrific. From then on, it's been downhill all the way.

His hobby is tropical fish. I hate tropical fish, Doctor. Not all tropical fish. Harry's tropical fish. There's something about them. Maybe it's the fact he talks to them. Or the names he gives them. Eric, Tony, Pinky. There's one round, mean-looking one he calls Dolly. When they die he buries them in the backyard. We're the only house in Larchmont with a tropical fish cemetery in the backyard.

I know it sounds crazy doctor but I hate those fish. I resent them in my living room and I resent them under my lawn. I'm a mature, sensible and, I think, rather intelligent woman and I hate those fish. How do you hate tropical fish?

You know something else I hate? Stereo equipment. Harry's got woofers, weefers, tweeters, baffles, pre-amps. He puts gloves on when he plays those records. White gloves like your friend.

Don't get me started, Doctor. There's so many things about Harry I hate.

Analysis: *Bad Habits*

Type: Comedic
Synopsis

Bad Habits is a wicked black comedy dealing with addiction, mental health, and the health care industry.

In act one Dolly comes to Ravenswood, a rehabilitation retreat for couples seeking therapy and relationship counseling, on a sudden urge to visit her husband, Harry. Harry has put himself under the care of Dr. Jason Pepper. Dolly has been reading Pepper's book on the subject, *Marriage for the Fun of It!* While most couples come to Ravenswood together, Harry came on his own, and has been here for months.

Dr. Pepper has been wheelchair-bound ever since his ex-wife threw him down a staircase. He runs the retreat with a fairly lax and mostly unorthodox hand. He encourages his patients to drink heavily, smoke heavily, and maintain high-calorie diets. Some of the patients here have been under his care for years. He treats all couples: male/female, male/male, female/female.

The outcome of his months of therapy is that Harry doesn't want to kill Dolly anymore.

Act two centers on Dunelawn, a facility for people battling addictions: drinking, smoking, dressing in drag. It is run by the always-silent Dr. Toynbee. He has two female nurses on staff who do all of the work; their names are Benson and Hedges. Hedges makes the observation that none of the patients here ever seem to get better. When the patients get the urge to act on their addictions, the nurses inject them with a serum that temporarily soothes the desire.

Character Description
Dolly Scrupp, 40s
Dolly's right foot is currently in an orthopedic shoe. She's been reading Dr. Pepper's book *Marriage for the Fun of It!* in hopes of getting closer to her husband, Harry. Harry is here alone because Dolly believes there is nothing wrong with her. They live in Larchmont, New York. Dolly doesn't drink alcohol or smoke. She only drinks water or diet soda. Harry ran over her foot while she was sunbathing, with a remote control lawnmower, breaking the second and third toes on the right. She is a housewife and mother. She has lost some weight since Harry checked in.

Harry reveals to Dr. Pepper a series of incident (accidents?) committed by Dolly that have left him hospitalized, in traction. The couple has pretty much been trying to kill each other since the day they married. In the end, Harry ends up checking out and going home while Dolly checks in.

Given Circumstances
Who are they? Dr. Pepper works at Ravenswood, where Dolly's husband is a patient.

Where are they? The grounds of the rehabilitation retreat.

When does this take place? The present.

Why are they there? Dolly has been reading the doctor's book and came to check in on Harry.

What is the pre-beat? Dr. Pepper asks Dolly what Harry is like in bed.

Questions
1. Can you state your objective in a simple, specific, and active way?
2. Who are you talking to? Be specific and have a clear image.
3. Can you think of three adjectives to describe your character?

4. How long have you and Harry been married?
5. What does he look like?
6. Have you missed him since he's been at Ravenswood?
7. Do you love him?
8. How many kids do the two of you have?
9. Is this what you thought married life would be like?
10. What made you pick up Dr. Pepper's book?
11. What spoke to you about it?
12. Is Dr. Pepper attractive?
13. Do you want him to fix your marriage?
14. When was the last time you and Harry had sex?
15. Have you ever cheated on him?

Elemeno Pea
Molly Smith Metzler

MICHAELA

I said Blue. *Blue Hydrangea*. Labor Day's over! I said to the florist on the phone, I said, No White. If you give me white . . . if you fucking give me white . . . and did she listen Simone?!

I obviously should've done the flowers myself but for some asinine reason, I thought it was more important to accompany my husband back to New York because for some asinine reason, I actually thought I . . . I thought we . . .

Why don't I have any shoes on?! I'm losing my mind now—

And my makeup's a mess now and I don't have my makeup bag; I don't have my Laura Mercier primer—

Because *Phil would not take the jet out until the fog cleared.* And Peter got all *Peter* about it and said he would therefore drive *himself* back to the city in his stupid Jaguar. So we left the airport and headed to the ferry station. But then we passed the Ice Cream Smuggler, and Peter said he wanted a sugar cone. So we pulled over, and he went in, but when he came out, he was empty-handed. So I said, "What happened honey? Did you lose interest in ice cream?" And he said "There were too many kids in there." And I said, "Well okay—I'll go in for you. What do you want?" And he said "What I want is for you to get the fuck out of my car." And he pulled over in the middle of traffic and pushed me out and slammed my car door shut and peeled out and left me standing there.

And all these cars were whizzing by me—and this Volkswagen stopped to see if I needed help—like I was some fucking homeless woman—and it was so humiliating, I just turned around and started running. I didn't even know where I was running to! And then I got your video, and I couldn't tell what the video was saying without the sound, but there you were, and you were waving at me, and I suddenly remembered you were *on* the island . . .

I didn't know what else to do, I just came here.

Analysis: *Elemeno Pea*

Type: Seriocomic
Synopsis

The action takes place on a beach estate, on a bluff, in Martha's Vineyard, just after Labor Day. There is a main house, a guest house, and servants' quarters. Michaela and Peter Kell are the owners of the estate, and Simone is Michaela's personal assistant. Michaela is letting Simone have a girls' weekend with her sister, Devon. Simone and Devon are staying in the guest house. It is equipped with voice-activated iTunes in the ceiling, and floor-to-ceiling glass walls that lead onto a wraparound porch with an amazing view. These people have a lot of money.

Simone and Devon are from Buffalo, New York. They are total opposites. Simone is beautiful, tan, and poised. She makes a lot of money working for Michaela and she is also writing a novel. Devon is at a low point in her life. Recently divorced, working a terrible low-paying job, and sleeping in her parents' basement, she is overwhelmed by the wealth here. Devon spends the play constantly reminding Simone that she is the "help" and that she's deserted her family on numerous occasions for strangers.

This is a world unlike any Simone and Devon have known. Devon doesn't understand Michaela or her sense of entitlement. She also doesn't understand how Simone has let Michaela bribe her with money, gifts, and trips in order to stay. Michaela is going through some really difficult marital trouble. She offers Devon a substantial amount of money ($10,000) to leave. Devon refuses, although she takes the check.

From that moment on, Devon uses every opportunity to undermine Michaela. She invites the groundskeeper, called Jos-B because there is another man named José who works on the property, to dinner. When Ethan walks in, Devon sizes him up immediately and realizes she knows nothing about her sister, who has seemed to abandon all her dreams on account of money.

When Michaela reveals to Devon the tragedy of her husband forcing her to get an abortion because tests showed something wrong with the baby, Devon finally sees her and the two find common ground. Simone, on the other hand, decides to go off on a boat trip with Ethan, leaving all the problems behind her.

Character Description
Michaela, early 40s
She's married to Peter Kell, whose family owns the estate. She's strikingly beautiful and impeccably groomed. Peter is CEO of an advertising company. His family is an institution. Michaela has a law degree from Yale but spends most of her time on charity and volunteer work. Money is no object to her. She paid Simone double overtime to work on Christmas and pays her a six-figure salary. She also made Simone sign a confidentiality agreement. Michaela left a huge gift basket filled with goodies for Devon in the bedroom. She admits Peter can be cruel to her; he picks on her. She is Peter's second wife. She has a psychic she consults frequently.

Given Circumstances

Who are they? Simone is Michaela's assistant, and Devon is Simone's sister.

Where are they? A beach estate on Martha's Vineyard.

When does this take place? The present, just after Labor Day.

Why are they there? Devon is visiting Simone for the weekend.

What is the pre-beat? Michaela has just run from town to the house because Peter left her stranded.

Questions

1. Can you state your objective in a simple, specific, and active way?
2. Who are you talking to? Be specific and have a clear image.
3. Can you think of three adjectives to describe your character?
4. How long have things been strained between you and Peter?
5. How long have you two been together?
6. Has Peter ever been this actively mean to you before?
7. Do you love him?
8. Do you think your marriage is salvageable?
9. Did you come from money, or marry into it?
10. Do you miss practicing law?
11. Are you good at managing the estate?
12. What does Simone mean to you?
13. Are you jealous of her relationship with Devon?
14. Do you find Devon's presence here a threat?
15. How can Simone fix this situation?

Bob
Peter Sinn Nachtrieb

I was finishing my Sunday night diner at the Bamboo Wok. I don't know how authentic or healthy it is but I like the flavors. I'd been working my way through the menu for about a year. Each week, I would have a new entrée in order of appearance. I'd finally made it to the "Noodles slash Rice" section after several months of Lamb and I felt like I was entering a new era in my life.

When the waiter delivered the check and cookie, the fortune inside seemed different. The paper looked shiny, almost golden, the ink darker, more insistent.

"You will be the mother to a great great man."

The fortunes I usually get are a little more vague than that. But this felt intentional. Like someone was watching me. From inside the cookie.

It made me smile. I thought "Well, cool, Jeanine, maybe the future isn't only selling tiny burgers and having Asian food once a week." And then my stomach started to twitch, felt like I was gonna be sick. I started sweating, breathing heavy. And I thought Oh my god, it's happening already. I stood up from my table and shouted "I'm gonna be the mother to a great great man!"

Next thing I knew I woke up in a hospital bed. At first I thought I'd conceived my great man immaculate until the nurse told me that I'd almost died at the restaurant. That I had a severe reaction to the gluten in Asian-noodles slash rice that messed up my insides so much that I would never be able to make a "Great Great Man" the regular way.

I don't really care for fortunes very much anymore. But, funny, you know, there you are. There you are.

Analysis: *Bob*

Type: Seriocomic
Synopsis

Bob is a five-act play that tells the story of one man's life from birth to old age. Each act has a title that tells the audience exactly what they're about to see. Jeanine appears in the play only briefly in act one, titled "How Bob is born, abandoned, raised by a fast food employee, discovers his dream, and almost dies."

Jeanine relates the above story about finding Bob. She decides to keep the baby and raise him as her own. Connor, Jeanine's ex-boyfriend and a policeman, gets tipped off about the baby from Helen, Bob's birthmother. Helen doesn't reveal her true identity. Connor shows up at Jeanine's house, but she denies knowing anything about the baby. She sends Connor away. Connor tells her he's still in love with her and one he'll prove himself. Jeanine take the baby, jumps in her car, and flees town.

Twelve years on, Bob and Jeanine find themselves in Chicago. Jeanine is exhausted. The constant running has finally caught up with her. She realizes she is dying and reveals to Bob that she's not his real mother. He builds her a funeral pyre on the steps of the Art Institute and is almost arrested by none other than Connor, now a Chicago policeman. Bob holds on to the last thing Jeanine said to him: "You can do anything you want with your life." He sets off alone and is immediately robbed of his money and clothes by Helen, his real mom, who doesn't recognize him.

Bob continues on his journey. He meets various people, has plenty of experiences, and learns a lesson from every encounter. Bob's life becomes a truly epic journey. He finally discovers Helen, who has married Connor, and she asks if he is a great man. He replies, "I'm smart, I'm well-meaning, and I'm pretty good at making love."

Character Description
Jeanine, 40s
Jeanine is an employee of White Castle in Louisville, Kentucky. She finds the baby Bob in the bathroom on Valentine's Day. She immediately consults the corporation's instruction manual to figure out what to do in such a situation. The first thing it says is not to look in the baby's eyes, which, of course, Jeanine does. She immediately falls in love with him and decides to raise him as her own. She does not call the police. She names him Bob. Actually, he pretty much names himself because the sound he makes is "bwaahhbb."

Jeanine used to date Connor, the local policeman. She owns a beige Chevy Malibu. Jeanine feels she has achieved little in life, so it's important to her that Bob know he can do anything he wants.

Given Circumstances
Who are they? Jeanine is relaying the story to Bob, a baby.
Where are they? Jeanine's car, driving away from Louisville, Kentucky.
When does this take place? The present.
Why are they there? Jeanine found the baby and kept him for herself.
What is the pre-beat? Jeanine tried not to look at Bob but did and fell in love.

Questions

1. Can you state your objective in a simple, specific, and active way?
2. Who are you talking to? Be specific and have a clear image.
3. Can you think of three adjectives to describe your character?
4. What does Bob look like?
5. Have you always wanted a baby?
6. Did you ever have the opportunity to get married?
7. How long have you been in Louisville?
8. What do you like about it?
9. How long have you worked at White Castle?
10. Is there anything about the job you liked?
11. Are you glad to have a reason to leave town?
12. How are you going to support a child?
13. Where are you driving to?
14. How will you explain the baby once you get somewhere?
15. What do you feel when you look at him?

Butterfly Kiss
Phyllis Nagy

JENNY

Lily, can you tell me what it is exactly a lepidopterist *does*? Honestly, when I met your daddy he was a soldier. He was just a regular guy. It was years later he took an interest in bugs.

I was reading up on the subject of butterflies in an encyclopedia yesterday. Really. I was. Sitting here in my old comfy chair while you were at school, reading, and listening to Billie Holiday, her sweet voice, and the telephone rings. Ring ring goes the phone and you know, for a long time I think it's part of Billie's song. A ringing telephone is such an unfamiliar sound to me, honey.

I can't get together the extra push, the rush of energy it takes to pull myself out of that chair. So I figure, why bother? It'll stop soon enough. But it doesn't stop. And so I throw all I've got into the act of getting up and I answer and the ringing stops and there's a voice. A female voice with an accent.

The voice says to my telephone: *Bonjour*. May I *parler* with Sloan Ross? I say to myself, Jenny, who the hell is Sloan Ross? The female voice is . . . nervous. I can tell by the breathing. Very quick. In spurts. And then I remember. Well, *yeah*, Sloan Ross is the father of my baby.

I try to answer the voice's question, but by that time it's gone. What's left for your mama to do but return to her chair?

It's a funny thing, Lily. When I met your daddy, I was a switchboard operator. The telephone was my line to excitement.

And I couldn't even keep a timid female voice on the line. Well.
It's better to sit in the dark and remember nothing. If you sit
in the dark long enough something scary's bound to happen.

Analysis: *Butterfly Kiss*

Type: Dramatic
Synopsis

The action of the play focuses on Lily Ross, a twenty-something
resident of New York City. Lily works at a small gift shop at the South
Street Seaport, but her real interest is musical composition. Lily grew
up on a matriarchal household surrounded by her mother and grand-
mother. At the opening of the play, Lily is in prison for allegedly
killing her mother.

The story bounces back and forth between the present and the
past as Nagy slowly reveals the depths of Lily's psyche and the hold
she has over the people in her life. Lily is an enigma, and everyone
wants her and wants to know more about her.

Lily spends her time in prison reading up on famous, sensational
murder cases. She then relays the stories to Martha, her lover, when
she visits. Lily tells Martha she wants to write an opera.

Sloan, Lily's father, is a lepidopterist, mostly absent, and has a
lover. Jenny, Lily's mother, stays home all day. Sloan may have
arranged for the barely teenaged Lily to seduce his best friend, Teddy,
because he likes to scientifically observe things.

Jenny treats Lily more like a sister than a daughter. Jenny's
generalized anxieties increase once she suspects Sloan of having
an affair. Jenny slowly starts to lose her mind. She asks the same
questions over and over. She believes Lily lives with a man. She
thinks Lily is pregnant and wants her to name the baby Jenny, after
her. She wants Lily to write songs for her.

One day, while Lily is brushing Jenny's hair, she takes Sloan's gun out of the bedside table and coaxes Jenny into asking for death. This scene is the final one in the play, and Nagy leaves it to the audience to decide whether Jenny wants to die or not.

Character Description
Jenny Ross, mid- to late 40s
Jenny is a mild hypochondriac, attractive, lusty, neurotically thin (but thinks she's fat), and blessed with a beautiful singing voice. She drinks scotch and constantly takes her blood pressure and keeps a chart of the results. She believes that the women in her family all inherited the booze gene. Jenny wants to be normal for Sloan so that he'll love her. She wishes she looked more like Tallulah Bankhead. Jenny always wears black, thinking she looks best in it—because Sloan said so. Sloan also told her, "Don't be so boring."

Jenny is desperately lonely. She tries to get Lily to dance with her just so someone will touch her. One of the reasons she takes her blood pressure is that she likes the firm feeling of the strap on her arm. Jenny tries to get Sloan to touch her, to see her, but he either ignores her or fucks her. Lily says Jenny isn't sick but "somewhere between pretending and death."

Given Circumstances
Who are they? Lily is Jenny's daughter.
Where are they? Jenny and Lily's home.
When does this take place? The present.
Why are they there? Jenny gets dressed up and then drinks a lot but doesn't leave the house.
What is the pre-beat? This is the top of the scene.

Questions

1. Can you state your objective in a simple, specific, and active way?
2. Who are you talking to? Be specific and have a clear image.
3. Can you think of three adjectives to describe your character?
4. How long have you and Sloan been married?
5. When is the last time you saw him?
6. Are you still in love with him?
7. What do you see when you look at Lily?
8. Do you love your daughter?
9. Why do you constantly take your blood pressure?
10. When was the last time you left the house?
11. When is the last time you made love?
12. What is your drink of choice?
13. What are you pretending to be?
14. How do you define "normal"?
15. Have you ever had an affair?

Madame Melville
Richard Nelson

CLAUDIE

Did you stay in the toilet until the others had left? Is that what you were doing?

You didn't hear the bell? You didn't hear Sophie's very loud mother?

You didn't know everyone was leaving?

You weren't trying—on purpose—to stay behind? I think you were, Carl. And—I think there is nothing remotely wrong with that. But then again maybe you didn't know why you were staying back. I think men often don't know what makes them do the things they do. I think that is why women find men so—dangerous.

And so—terrible.

And of course men find women dangerous for totally different reasons. Isn't that true?

We were talking about just this in class this week, weren't we? Drink your Orangina. The books women have written about men—such as they are, and those by men about women. How different they are. It wasn't exactly on the curriculum, I snuck it in. Very bold of me, wasn't it? I looked to you two or three times in the discussion to join us. To tell us what you know about what men think about women. You must know a lot.

Don't you?

Next time—participate. Still I'm so happy you're in my class. So nice to see your attentive face there. Though I keep wanting to push that hair back.

Analysis: *Madame Melville*

Type: Seriocomic
Synopsis
The action takes place in 1966 in the Paris apartment of Madame Claudie Melville. It's a time when the world was about to explode. Claudie teaches literature at the American School.

After one of Claudie's movie nights, Carl finds himself alone in the apartment with her. They've just gone to see the very famous surfing movie *The Endless Summer*. Claudie teases Carl that he didn't like it as much as the French films about sex. Carl, although young and slightly unsure, stands his ground regarding his opinion on the film. Claudie tells him he's smart but could still do better in her class. She wants him to assert himself more. Claudie asks Carl if he didn't, perhaps, stay in the bathroom while people were leaving so that he would, in fact, be left alone here with her.

Claudie takes cigarettes from Carl. She lies on the couch with her feet pressed up against him. They drink wine together. Suddenly the lines between teacher and student begin to blur. Carl asks her questions about her life, along with questions regarding art, music, and literature. He's hungry for knowledge.

Circumstances necessitate Carl spending the night at Claudie's apartment. Claudie calls his mother, who approves, under the (incorrect) assumption that Madame Melville is married. They sleep together.

The next day Ruth comes over and spends time with the two. She quickly catches on to what's happened between them but reserves judgment. Claudie takes Carl to the Louvre and shows him her favorite, and least favorite, paintings. His education continues.

The two return to the apartment later on Saturday. Ruth tells them Carl's mother came by. The headmaster gave her the address.

The three spend the evening talking more about art and music until Carl's father arrives and, with barely a scene, brings the boy home.

Carl's parents make plans to send him back to Ohio. On his last night in Paris he arranges for them to take him to dinner close to Madame Melville's apartment. He uses the excuse of going to the bathroom to run to her apartment. They sit on Claudie's sofa and she plays *The Magic Flute* for them. Claudie, on her way to a date, asks Carl to wait until she leaves before he exits her apartment.

Character Description
Claudie Melville, early 40s

Claudie teaches literature at the American School in Paris. She invites a small group of students out to the movies twice a week, and then they discuss the films. Her apartment is filled with books. She smokes. She hates ties on young men. She tells Carl they'll have to train his hair to lay right. She listens to all the current music of the day, popular and jazz. Claudie doesn't like Carl's father because when he came to visit the school he laughed when explaining that Carl wants to be a poet one day. She responded by telling him the world needed all the poets it could get. She tells Carl to be a playwright because we all need an audience. She is Catholic. Ruth, her friend and neighbor, is an American musician. She's in the middle of a rocky relationship with Paul Darc, the math teacher at school.

Given Circumstances

Who are they? Carl is Claudie's fifteen-year-old American student.
Where are they? The living room of Claudie's Paris apartment.
When does this take place? 1966.
Why are they there? It's one of Claudie's film and discussion nights.
What is the pre-beat? They've been listening to music, and Claudie has a realization.

Questions

1. Can you state your objective in a simple, specific, and active way?
2. Who are you talking to? Be specific and have a clear image.
3. Can you think of three adjectives to describe your character?
4. What's your opinion of Carl been up until tonight?
5. Has he done anything in particular to get your attention up until now?
6. Have any other students ever pulled this staying-behind trick before?
7. Have you ever slept with any of your students before?
8. Do you find Carl attractive?
9. Are you doing this because you're mad at Paul?
10. Do you enjoy teaching?
11. What books are on your list of favorites?
12. Is it different teaching American students versus French?
13. How much money do you make a year?
14. How long have you been in your apartment?
15. Has life turned out the way you expected it to when you were fifteen?

Playing with Grown Ups
Hannah Patterson

JOANNA

I don't think I want her, Robert.

I don't. I don't think I want her. I mean I wasn't sure, before, but I assumed, I hoped, it would all just fall into place. And suddenly I would. But it hasn't. Not at all.

I was in the car, Robert. Yesterday. Or the day before. I don't know, with the days . . . It was at the supermarket. In the car park. And she was in the back, screaming. And screaming. And screaming. For no reason. I'd given her everything she could want. I'd fed her. I'd held her.

She made me feel sick. The smell of her. And she wouldn't be comforted. And I sat there, for hours and hours, it felt like. Staring at the wall in front of me. The big, flat, concrete wall. And it seemed to present an answer, all of a sudden. And I thought, if I reverse the car, now, and I put it into gear, I could just slam my foot down, hard and fast, on the accelerator, and ram it right into that wall. And then it would all stop, just for a moment.

So, you don't know, do you, how I feel?

Analysis: *Playing with Grown Ups*

Type: Dramatic
Synopsis

Joanna and Robert have just had a baby nine weeks ago. Robert works all day while Joanna is home with Lily. Things are tense between the two as they try to juggle their new way of life. Joanna is tired all the time and trying to lose the baby weight; she also may be drinking more wine than she should.

Robert has run into their friend Jake and invited him over for dinner without asking Joanna. Joanna isn't dressed or prepared for company. She doesn't consider Jake her friend anymore. When Jake appears with the much younger Stella, Joanna throws Robert an "I told you so" look. The new parents try to act like everything is okay in the house. Joanna is also an academic whose field of study is women who've been written out of history, which is perhaps how she's feeling now that she's had a baby and put her professional life on hold.

As the evening goes on, Stella surprises everyone with how smart, intuitive, and probing her mind is. In a way, she's the most grown up of anyone there. Robert is jealous of Jake's relationship and condemning of it. Joanna continues to drink too much and forgets to turn the oven on for dinner.

Robert knows that his department is under financial strain. Jake's monologue drives home the fact that his job is at stake and he should, perhaps, be looking for another job. When Robert and Stella go to check on the crying baby, Jake tries to rekindle his old romance with Joanna. She admits she's made a terrible mistake.

Stella and Jake crash on the sofa, and Robert has a bit of a meltdown. The stress of everything is too much for him, and Jake gets the brunt of his anger. Lily starts crying, and Joanna makes Robert take her out of the apartment. Stella is the one who soothes everyone back into place.

Joanna finally admits that her career is more important to her then her family. The dead women she's trying to restore to the world mean more to her than the living child in the other room. She leaves.

Character Description

Joanna, 40

Joanna gave birth to Lily nine weeks and two days ago. She listens to Helen Reddy's "I Am Woman" on her iPod so loudly that she can't hear the baby crying on the monitor. She's already started drinking, although she probably shouldn't because she's breastfeeding. Joanna is an academic. Her field of study is neglected female writers who've been written out of history. She's desperate to go back to work. She and Jake once had a romantic relationship.

Given Circumstances

Who are they? Robert and Joanna are married and have recently had a baby.

Where are they? Their apartment.

When does this take place? The present.

Why are they there? Jake and Stella have just run out to pick up pizzas for dinner.

What is the pre-beat? Robert has told her to get some sleep and she'll gain some perspective.

Questions

1. How long have Joanna and Robert been a couple?
2. How did her relationship with Jake affect this relationship?
3. Was she ever truly in love with Robert?
4. How exactly does she feel he trapped her into having a baby?

5. How long has it been since she's worked?
6. What is it about her job that interests her most?
7. When she was a child, what did she imagine her life would be like?
8. When she looks at Robert, what does she feel?
9. When she looks at herself in the mirror, what does she see/feel?
10. How difficult is it for her to care for Lily?
11. Does she still want Jake?
12. Is she jealous of Stella?
13. Did she have a difficult pregnancy/labor/delivery?
14. What does she feel when singing along to Helen Reddy?
15. How much has she been drinking?

A Numbers Game
Tanya Saracho

ONE

My boyfriend, he doesn't know what to do with me, because even though he tells me that I look fine to him, fine is not enough to me. Do you know what fine means? Fine means, I'll fucking tolerate you. That's what fine means.

Fine means, "Sure, but could we please turn the lights off so I don't have to look at you?" Fine means "Our days are counted, baby unless you do something about your weight." Fine is people looking at you when you put anything in your mouth because all of a sudden you've turned into a social pariah. I sat there yesterday at a restaurant, and these two assholes were having some kind of a ball over at their table as I was trying to eat my freakin' lunch.

The two actually sat there staring at me, as I put the sandwich in my mouth. It was so embarrassing. I'm sitting there alone, which I hate in the first place, and these two douchebags are like whispering something—I notice cuz they're giggling like little girls over there. So I look and they don't really stop.

I try to ignore them but I mean, I have to freakin' eat my food, right? I have 45 minutes for lunch, I have to eat this thing. And I can feel their freakin' eyes on me, like burning across the restaurant and I say fuck it and take another bite and they . . . These two jerks makes this noise. Like . . .

(*Beat.*)

And I know what that noise is. I know what it means.
How did I let it get this bad?

Analysis: *A Numbers Game*

Type: Dramatic
Synopsis and Character Description

This monologue comes from a very short play that was part of Humana Festival's 2012 collection of plays and monologues centered around food and all of its complexities performed under the title *Oh, Gastronomy!*

Two females (One and Two) and one male (Three) speak directly to the audience. They are aware of each other, but they do not interact. One holds a bag of marbles in her hand and has a fishbowl in front of her. Every time she says a number, she drops a marble in the bowl.

The marbles correspond with gaining weight, each marble equaling a pound. One says the first goes unnoticed. In fact, the first five can go undetected. It could be water weight making the scale go up a little every day. It's not until you gain seven or eight pounds that it really becomes apparent. And then when people start to comment on it is when it's really a problem.

Your face starts to look different. You begin to feel different. Then you gain fifteen pounds and you have to buy new pants. One tries a cleanse diet involving cayenne pepper. It doesn't work. One tries Zumba and other fitness trends, but the weight still keeps coming. She feels like she's gaining weight by just breathing. One begins to move differently. She begins to wear more sweatshirts. She doesn't recognize herself in the mirror. Suddenly she's gained thirty pounds and she doesn't want to have sex because she feels ugly.

One feels like she's had no control over this situation.

Given Circumstances

Who are they? One is talking to the audience.

Where are they? She could be anywhere—it's up to you.

When does this take place? The present.

Why are they there? She's dealing with weight issues.

What is the pre-beat? She's just recounted her weight gain and feels disgusted by it.

Questions

1. Can you state your objective in a simple, specific, and active way?
2. Who are you talking to? Be specific and have a clear image.
3. Can you think of three adjectives to describe your character?
4. "The audience" isn't specific enough. Who could you be speaking to?
5. Where could this conversation be taking place?
6. You've put on almost thirty pounds. How?
7. What are all the things in your life that make you unhappy enough that you turn to food?
8. What does your boyfriend look like?
9. How long have you two been together?
10. Is he overweight? In shape?
11. How do *you* feel about your body?
12. Have you gained weight before, or is the first time?
13. How has it affected other facets of your life?
14. How many diets have you been on? Which ones?
15. Do you think you can actually fix the problem?

Getting Back to Mother
Kathryn Walat

MIMI

I was a bad waitress for a very long time. Over ten years, which is a long time to do something that you hate. I tried to get other, more menial jobs. I applied to Dunkin Donuts three times. I even interviewed once for this job where all you had to do is sit in a trailer and *count* things. But I couldn't get any of those jobs. Maybe people saw I had a college education—and I do point out it was state school, not even the good branch, and it took me six years to get my degree—maybe that makes them think I'm ambitious, that I didn't want repetitive, mind-numbing work, but really, I really do.

Eventually I got put on breakfast shift. Essentially you're inserting an intravenous of caffeine, customer after customer—dirty work. And you might not be able to guess this by looking at me, but I'm not a morning person. In fact, right now? It's actually 11 pm, that's why I look so lively. I'm just getting warmed up. But for the breakfast shift, I had to be there at five—I had to ride my bike because I didn't have a car then—or now—so I'm riding my bike through the city streets at 4:30 am, waving to the working girls as they drag their tired hoochies home. Naturally by three in the afternoon, I was ready to hit the bars. I had to start drinking with the old men and alkies, that dangerous overlapping Venn diagram. My friends stopped calling, they got sick of waking me up. I got sick of waiting for them to get off work. I basically dropped out of normally functioning society. It's then that I decided to go back to school to get my PhD in linguistics. Which I did, everything but the dissertation. I gave up. Met a guy, moved to the middle of nowhere with him—he's had a part-time, visiting professor gig for about twelve years. But Luke is always encouraging me to figure out what it is that I *really* want to do.

Which is how I get to my mother. Which is what I'm really supposed to be talking about here, right? Because I think it's safe—and fair, actually, if you hear me out—to say that *she's* the reason all I can really do is become a writer.

Which brings me back to the waitressing. I was such a *bad* waitress people could pretty easily get the sense that this was not my true calling. Sometimes, perhaps as they were on the fence about whether to give me a pity tip or not, they would ask: You a writer or something? My friend would get: You an actress? But I'm too ugly for that. But at the time, when they would ask me that, I'd say: No, I'm a waitress, the donut shop didn't want me. They'd sometimes probe further: You got kids? Thinking I had gotten knocked up, had four mouths to feed. I'd say: Nope, just looking for beer money—for *myself*.

Analysis: *Getting Back to Mother*

Type: Seriocomic
Synopsis and Character Description

This piece was written as a stand-alone monologue, so all of the factual information you need about the character and events can be found within.

Mimi is a woman in her forties who seems to have been living on the unlucky side of life for quite some time now. The title of the piece is called *Getting Back to Mother*, yet we're given very little information about Mimi's mother. All we know about her really is that she's the reason Mimi can become a writer. Mimi doesn't even admit that she is a writer. She says she "can be" and that people ask her if she is, but she never claims the title for herself. In the end, the only job Mimi takes ownership over is being a waitress, and a bad one at that.

So what is it about Mimi's mother and lack of information about her that leads her to this discovery?

It's lucky that Mimi landed a job as a waitress because she hasn't been able to land more menial jobs. It's unlucky that she has to work the morning shift because she's a night person. Even though she's college-educated, she wants a repetitive, mind-numbing job. What goes on in her mind that she needs/wants to numb it? She puts herself and her education down in her brief description of the state school and explaining that it took her six years to graduate.

It seems like she became an alcoholic for a while, drinking as soon as her shift was over and falling asleep before her friends were even home from their jobs. But she eventually picked herself up and got back into school—unfortunately, without the follow-through to graduate. Instead she put herself into the hands of a man and gave up her own sense of direction. Luke, her boyfriend, appears to be supportive, but Mimi is the one lacking drive. She thinks she's ugly.

The facts and the language leads me to believe that Mimi's lack of drive and lack of confidence in herself leads back to her relationship with her mother. It's up to you to craft the very specific road that took her there and why she's unable to talk about it. Her statement, "Which is what I'm really supposed to be talking about here, right?" leads me to believe that she is in therapy at the moment trying to work all of this out.

Given Circumstances

Who are they? As it's unspecified in the text, it's up to you to decide who Mimi is talking to. A therapist? An interviewer? A friend?

Where are they? It's not specified, so it depends on who you choose to be speaking to.

When does this take place? The present.

Why are they there? It's not specified, so you need to decide.

What is the pre-beat? As it's a stand-alone piece, you need to make a decision.

Questions

1. Can you state your objective in a simple, specific, and active way?
2. Who are you talking to? Be specific and have a clear image.
3. Can you think of three adjectives to describe your character?
4. Are you actively writing anything at the moment?
5. What issues, themes, types of characters do you usually explore in your writing?
6. What makes a good waitress?
7. What specifically makes you a bad waitress?
8. Have you tried to be a better waitress?
9. Why have "menial jobs" been your goal?
10. Where did you go to school?
11. Why did it take six years to get your degree?
12. Are you lonely?
13. What does Luke look like?
14. Are you in love with him?
15. Does your mom consider you successful, or a failure?

Brontosaurus
Lanford Wilson

ANTIQUES DEALER

I read somewhere that every ounce of alcohol you drink kills four thousand brain cells which are not regenerated. Contrary to what I read somewhere else.

I understand that rather than being a steady, every-night tippler, it's healthier, or less destructive, really, to go on a monthly all out binge. Which is worth considering if one is interested in being less destructive. Which maybe I am; despite appearances.

Nephew of mine, my house is yours.

Please make friends. Bring them here. I like young people. I like people, though I don't seem to sometimes. "People," you understand, no specific person. Bring them here. The "apartment" is yours. It's been photographed for every classy publication from Abitare to the Sunday Times Magazine and in not one picture has there been a living soul. Large, flat colorless rooms in perfect order. Flowers on every table and lovely, longing, sad-looking rooms.

I've never liked a single photograph. If you hate it here I'll help you find an apartment, but I hope you won't. And next spring maybe you can help me look for a house — in the country. It's past time. I don't want to live in the city. I've not found myself in the catalogues.

In the winter I tell myself I have to be here for the shop, but I need a summer place where I can get away. Only I'm chicken. I want land but I see myself buying a lush seven acres and with my care watching it turn to burning desert all around me. Within weeks.

Analysis: *Brontosaurus*

Type: Seriocomic
Synopsis and Character Description

Note: The role of the Antiques Dealer can be played by either a man or a woman.

The action of the play takes place in present-day New York City. The play opens with the Antiques Dealer waiting for the arrival of his/her nephew. The Dealer, late forties, is relating to his/her assistant the plot to the movie *The Little Shop of Horrors*. The Dealer explains to the assistant how, much like the plant, s/he's looking for someone to "feed me, sustain me, make me believe." S/he doesn't mention anything about being a killer like the infamous Audrey 2.

The Dealer's sister says that the Nephew is a puppy dog. S/he's just happy to have someone around to talk to all the time, although s/he's pretty sure s/he'll turn the young boy homosexual.

The Dealer refers to her/himself as myopic, filled with an enormous hope that is general and vast and unspecific. S/he is also extremely verbose, almost never stops talking, like a speed freak. While s/he may be along in years, s/he's a moral adolescent.

The Nephew is four hours late, and the Dealer is very worried. The Dealer dismisses the assistant, there is a jump in time, and suddenly the Nephew is there. The Dealer's verbal assault begins immediately and s/he tells the Nephew not to be scared, s/he's all protective coloring; a facade.

The Dealer drinks Manhattans and asks the Nephew to fix one, but the Nephew doesn't know what that is. The Nephew, here to study theology at NYU, is a threatening, almost dangerous presence whose entire being is the opposite of the Dealer's. The Dealer admits s/he can't even keep a plant alive.

Time passes. The Dealer and the Nephew cohabitate, but as strangers. The Dealer can't get them to eat or spend any time together and it drives him/her crazy. They two finally have some time together, and the Nephew recounts the moment in which he knew he had to become a minister. The Nephew then explains he's leaving to go live with friends; he had never intended on staying. The Nephew leaves, and the Dealer realizes s/he will be alone forever.

Given Circumstances
Who are they? The Dealer is talking to his/her seventeen-year-old nephew.
Where are they? The Dealer's NYC apartment.
When does this take place? The present.
Why are they there? The Nephew is staying here while he attends college.
What is the pre-beat? The Dealer asked if the Nephew's Methodist parents drink alcohol.

Questions
1. Can you state your objective in a simple, specific, and active way?
2. Who are you talking to? Be specific and have a clear image.
3. Can you think of three adjectives to describe your character?
4. Did you ever want children of your own?
5. Are you excited about having your nephew here with you?
6. What is his name?

7. What does he look like?
8. Does he make you nervous?
9. Where in New York is your apartment?
10. Is your shop in the same building?
11. How big is your business?
12. How much money do you make a year?
13. What do you enjoy most about antiques?
14. Do you drink a lot?
15. When is the last time you saw your sister?

Breakfast at the Track
Lanford Wilson

S

After however many years of marriage, you have not yet realized that you are a morning person. That you require four hours sleep and I require a minimum of eight. I do not wake up. I must carefully re-connect my spine every morning. Vertebra by vertebra. My eyes do not open. You wake up ready for the day and I wake up ready for the grave. Please do not do this. Good night. Good morning.

I will kill. There will be a former husband and a widow. I'll be in prison. I'll get some rest.

You do exactly the same thing. Only you do it at the other end of the day. We go to a party. At the stroke of ten forty-five you start to unbutton your spine, bone by fucking bone. I can see it happening. You start at the butt and work up to your neck and then your head begins to nod and you get a martyred expression on your face. Till I agree to be your crutch on the way home. Don't give me you don't understand, you do the same thing. We're home by eleven-fifteen every night, you're asleep by eleven-seventeen.

Out cold. Always.

Analysis: *Breakfast at the Track*

Type: Seriocomic
Synopsis and Character Description

Breakfast at the Track is a very short play that takes place in a Saratoga Springs hotel room on the 14th of August at 6:30 am.

S and H are a long-married couple. H is a morning person, and S is most decidedly not. She feels him stir in bed and, thinking something's wrong, begins the play with a simple, "Who's there?" H says it's time to get up and start the day. S thinks it's still the middle of the night. H read and fell asleep at round 1:30, and S stayed up later. They have to get started because they're having breakfast at the track.

S would like to sleep for a full eight hours. She would like H not to ask her what time she actually fell asleep and what she was reading before she did so. They came here on vacation for sunshine, excitement, music, and horse racing. H feels that S spends every waking hour asleep and every sleeping hour in bed reading. They are not happy with each other.

S thinks H is sick for getting up so early on vacation to see the sunrise and go to a 7:00 a.m. breakfast. Vacation, to S, means sleeping in and relaxing. She thinks his obsessive attention to detail is neurotic.

The spat escalates until H says it's late and he has to shower if he's going to make it. S dozes off again, and H calls out, asking if she's getting up, waking her up.

Given Circumstances

Who are they? S and H are married.
Where are they? A Saratoga Springs, New York, hotel room.
When does this take place? The present, 6:30 a.m.
Why are they there? They are on vacation.
What is the pre-beat? H has just said he'll go to breakfast by himself.

Questions

1. Can you state your objective in a simple, specific, and active way?
2. Who are you talking to? Be specific and have a clear image.
3. Can you think of three adjectives to describe your character?
4. How long have you and H been married?
5. What is H's full name?
6. Are you still in love with him?
7. What is his most attractive feature?
8. What is his most annoying habit?
9. Do you have children? How many? How old?
10. What is H's career? Yours?
11. Are you two well-off?
12. Is this a nice hotel?
13. How long is your vacation?
14. How many times have you had this particular fight?
15. What makes this time different?

Say de Kooning
Lanford Wilson

WILLIE

I'm a wreck. I'm an idiot. I'm crazy to even be out here.

I left the damn city early, which was the popular thing to do as everybody else decided to—you've never seen traffic like that. It looked like Dean and Deluca was giving something away.

I loathe Long Island. I loathe the L.I.E. It is flat, boring, badly planned, hot and under repair. With all the goddamned local traffic weaving on and off.

I understand what's-his-name drove off the damn thing again last week and hit another tree. Out of sheer boredom probably. If they don't take his license away there won't be a tree left standing on the island.

It took me thirty-eight minutes in a driving cloudburst to get from the light to the Monument. And in that mood I had to charm some local, cocky, smirking seventeen-year-old total delinquent into parting with one of the four hundred empty cardboard boxes he was gloating over. Can you imagine me charming and coquettish?

Well I was. Had anyone I work with seen me they would have thrown up.

Analysis: *Say de Kooning*

Type: Comedic
Synopsis and Character Description

The action of the play takes place on a Friday afternoon of Labor Day Weekend in the living room of a house on the East End of Long Island. There are cardboard boxes all over the room.

Willie is approximately forty-five-years years old, strong, dynamic, and controlled. Bob refers to her as "butch and belligerent." She has just dug up a plant with her bare hands because she couldn't find the shovel, and now she's bleeding. She was pulling up the rosemary and the African daisy from the garden.

The summer apparently did not go well for Willie; a washout. Bob and Willie share a brandy and try to make conversation, but there is tension in the air. Willie works for the city as a psychiatrist. She spends all week with prisoners. She's only been to the rental twice this summer, sharing it with Bob (twenty-five years old) and Mandy (just under thirty).

Bob is an artist. He draws in pen and ink, brush, pencil. Willie has a big drawing of his in her office. Willie is a little hysterical about settling up for the summer, which motivates her opening monologue, and Bob is a little hysterical because he has no home in New York to go back to. His former lover took the money Bob gave him to pay rent and utilities.

Mandy and Willie are lovers—only Mandy has spent the summer avoiding Willie.

The Village Voice just did a profile on Willie and called her "The Last Angry Young Man in America." Willie thinks if she ever relaxes she'll unravel like a sweater.

Mandy finally arrives and the situation gets even more tense. Willie admits she finds her job debilitating and useless. Mandy won't admit

where she's been all week. Finally Mandy admits she took a new job.
She wants a respectable job for Willie's sake.

Willie has ambitions of being appointed Health Commissioner.
Mandy is trying to help her.

The three go off to a party to promote Willie and celebrate the
end of the summer, tensions between them somewhat eased.

Given Circumstances

Who are they? Bob and Willie are in a summer house share
together.

Where are they? The house, on the East End of Long Island.

When does this take place? The present, Friday of Labor Day
Weekend.

Why are they there? They're packing up the house for the season.

What is the pre-beat? Willie just dug up two plants from the garden
with her hands.

Questions

1. Can you state your objective in a simple, specific, and active
   way?
2. Who are you talking to? Be specific and have a clear image.
3. Can you think of three adjectives to describe your character?
4. What about Bob do you not like?
5. Is he a good artist?
6. How did the two of you meet?
7. What kept you from coming here most of the summer?
8. What does it mean to be a psychiatrist?
9. What is your job for the city?
10. Do you find it fulfilling?
11. How much money do you make a year?
12. What are all the pressures keeping you strung together?

13. What does Mandy look like?
14. How long have you two been together?
15. What in her behavior is making you question the future of your relationship?

ACKNOWLEDGMENTS

To all my teachers and mentors—there are almost too many to name—who had a hand in shaping my view on theater and how I teach it: Helen White, Jim Carnahan, Nicky Martin, Rob Marshall, Sam Mendes, John Crowley, David Leveaux, Susan Bristow, and Amy Saltz.

To the people who read and advised initial drafts of the book: Dennis Flanagan, David A. Miller, and Saidah Arrika Ekulona.

To Katya Campbell for introducing me to more up-and-coming playwrights that the world needs to know.

To all the playwrights and agents represented here, for their permission.

To Mom, Dad, and Joe.

PLAY SOURCES AND ACKNOWLEDGMENTS

Breakfast at the Track by Lanford Wilson. Copyright © 1983 by Lanford Wilson. Used by permission of ICM Partners. All inquiries should be addressed to ICM Partners, 730 Fifth Avenue, 4th Floor, New York, NY 10019.

Brontosaurus by Lanford Wilson. Copyright © 1977 by Lanford Wilson. Used by permission of ICM Partners. All inquiries should be addressed to ICM Partners, 730 Fifth Avenue, 4th Floor, New York, NY 10019.

Brooklyn Boy by Donald Margulies. Copyright © © 2005 by Donald Margulies. Published by Theatre Communications Group. Used by permission of Theatre Communications Group. All inquiries should be addressed to Theatre Communications Group, 520 8th Avenue, 24th Floor, New York, NY 10018

Burnt Orange by Lila Feinberg. Copyright © 2011 by Lila Feinberg. All inquiries should be addressed to Ron West at Thruline Entertainment, west@thrulinela.com or westasst@thrulinela.com.

Butterfly Kiss by Phyllis Nagy. Used by permission of Nick Hern Books. All inquiries should be addressed to Performing Rights Manager, Nick Hern Books, The Glasshouse, 49a Goldhawk Road, London W12 8QP (info@nickhernbooks.co.uk).

Death Tax by Lucas Hnath. Copyright © 2012 by Lucas Hnath. Used by permission of ICM Partners. All inquiries should be addressed to ICM Partners, 730 Fifth Avenue, 4th Floor, New York, NY 10019.

More Titles from The Applause Acting Series

How I Did It
Establishing a Playwriting
Career
edited by Lawrence Harbison
9781480369634...............$24.99

25 10-Minute Plays
for Teens
edited by Lawrence Harbison
9781480387768...............$16.99

More 10-Minute Plays
for Teens
edited by Lawrence Harbison
9781495011801..................$9.99

10-Minute Plays for Kids
edited by Lawrence Harbison
9781495053399..................$9.99

On Singing Onstage
by David Craig
9781557830432...............$18.99

The Stanislavsky
Technique: Russia
by Mel Gordon
9780936839080...............$16.95

Speak with Distinction
*by Edith Skinner/Revised with
New Material Added by Timothy
Monich and Lilene Mansell*
9781557830470...............$39.99

Recycling Shakespeare
by Charles Marowitz
9781557830944...............$14.95

Acting in Film
by Michael Caine
9781557832771...............$19.99

The Actor and the Text
by Cicely Berry
9781557831385...............$22.99

The Craftsmen
of Dionysus
by Jerome Rockwood
9781557831552...............$19.99

A Performer Prepares
by David Craig
9781557833952...............$19.99

Directing the Action
by Charles Marowitz
9781557830722...............$18.99

Acting in Restoration
Comedy
by Simon Callow
9781557831194...............$18.99

Shakespeare's Plays
in Performance
by John Russell Brown
9781557831361...............$18.99

The Shakespeare Audition
How to Get Over Your Fear,
Find the Right Piece, and
Have a Great Audition
by Laura Wayth
9781495010804...............$16.99

OTHER ACTING TITLES AVAILABLE

The Monologue Audition
A Practical Guide for Actors
by Karen Kohlhaas
9780879102913...............$22.99

The Scene Study Book
Roadmap to Success
by Bruce Miller
9780879103712...............$16.99

Acting Solo
Roadmap to Success
by Bruce Miller
9780879103750...............$16.99

Actor's Alchemy
Finding the Gold in the Script
by Bruce Miller
9780879103835...............$16.99

Stella Adler – The Art
of Acting
*compiled & edited by
Howard Kissel*
9781557833730...............$29.99

Acting with Adler
by Joanna Rotté
9780879102982...............$16.99

Accents
A Manual for Actors –
Revised & Expanded Edition
by Robert Blumenfeld
9780879109677...............$29.99

Acting with the Voice
The Art of Recording Books
by Robert Blumenfeld
9780879103019...............$19.95

AN IMPRINT OF
HAL•LEONARD
www.halleonardbooks.com

Monologue and Scene Books

Best Contemporary Monologues for Kids Ages 7-15
edited by Lawrence Harbison
9781495011771 .... $16.99

Best Contemporary Monologues for Men 18-35
edited by Lawrence Harbison
9781480369610 .... $16.99

Best Contemporary Monologues for Women 18-35
edited by Lawrence Harbison
9781480369627 .... $16.99

Best Monologues from The Best American Short Plays, Volume Three
edited by William W. Demastes
9781480397408 .... $19.99

Best Monologues from The Best American Short Plays, Volume Two
edited by William W. Demastes
9781480385481 .... $19.99

Best Monologues from The Best American Short Plays, Volume One
edited by William W. Demastes
9781480331556 .... $19.99

The Best Scenes for Kids Ages 7-15
edited by Lawrence Harbison
9781495011795 .... $16.99

Childsplay
A Collection of Scenes and Monologues for Children
edited by Kerry Muir
9780879101886 .... $16.99

Duo!: The Best Scenes for Mature Actors
edited by Stephen Fife
9781480360204 .... $19.99

Duo!: The Best Scenes for Two for the 21st Century
edited by Joyce E. Henry, Rebecca Dunn Jaroff, and Bob Shuman
9781557837028 .... $19.99

Duo!: Best Scenes for the 90's
edited by John Horvath, Lavonne Mueller, and Jack Temchin
9781557830302 .... $18.99

In Performance: Contemporary Monologues for Teens
by JV Mercanti
9781480396616 .... $16.99

In Performance: Contemporary Monologues for Men and Women Late Teens to Twenties
by JV Mercanti
9781480331570 .... $18.99

In Performance: Contemporary Monologues for Men and Women Late Twenties to Thirties
by JV Mercanti
9781480367470 .... $16.99

Men's Comedic Monologues That Are Actually Funny
edited by Alisha Gaddis
9781480396814 .... $14.99

One on One: The Best Men's Monologues for the 21st Century
edited by Joyce E. Henry, Rebecca Dunn Jaroff, and Bob Shuman
9781557837011 .... $18.99

One on One: The Best Women's Monologues for the 21st Century
edited by Joyce E. Henry, Rebecca Dunn Jaroff, and Bob Shuman
9781557837004 .... $18.99

One on One: The Best Men's Monologues for the Nineties
edited by Jack Temchin
9781557831514 .... $12.95

One on One: The Best Women's Monologues for the Nineties
edited by Jack Temchin
9781557831521 .... $11.95

One on One: Playing with a Purpose
Monologues for Kids Ages 7-15
edited by Stephen Fife and Bob Shuman with contribuing editors Eloise Rollins-Fife and Marit Shuman
9781557838414 .... $16.99

One on One: The Best Monologues for Mature Actors
edited by Stephan Fife
9781480360198 .... $19.99

Scenes and Monologues of Spiritual Experience from the Best Contemporary Plays
edited by Roger Ellis
9731480331563 .... $19.99

Scenes and Monologues from Steinberg/ATCA New Play Award Finalists, 2008-2012
edited by Bruce Burgun
9781476868783 ... $19.99

Soliloquy!
The Shakespeare Monologues
edited by Michael Earley and Philippa Keil
9780936839783
Men's Edition $12.99
9780936839790
Women's Edition $14.95

Teen Boys' Comedic Monologues That Are Actually Funny
edited by Alisha Gaddis
9781480396791 .... $14.99

Teens Girls' Comedic Monologues That Are Actually Funny
edited by Alisha Gaddis
9781480396807 .... $14.99

Women's Comedic Monologues That Are Actually Funny
edited by Alisha Gaddis
9781480360426 ...... $14.99

APPLAUSE THEATRE & CINEMA BOOKS
AN IMPRINT OF
HAL•LEONARD®
www.halleonardbooks.com

Prices, contents, and availability subject to change without notice.